CONTENTS

Twenty-three-year-old Private Eric Derwent Fletcher of the 2nd Carmarthenshire (Llanelli) Battalion Home Guard, photographed by his friend Herbert Grice on 24 August 1940. The Home Guard, it was suggested in one post-war eulogy, combined '. . . the courage of the lion with the gentle grace of the dove'.

THE HOME GUARD

DAVID CARROLL

SUTTON PUBLISHING LIMITED

Sutton Publishing Limited
Phoenix Mill · Thrupp · Stroud
Gloucestershire · GL5 2BU

First published 1999

Cover photographs (clockwise from top right): Busmen LDVs at a London Transport depot, 1940; a young lady Home Guard Auxiliary at the wheel of an Upper Thames Patrol motor launch, 1940; a Southern Railway porter being trained to use a rifle by a soldier from the Regular Army, 1940; a contingent of the East Lancashire Home Guard, 1940. (All photographs appear with permission of the Trustees of the Imperial War Museum, London).

British Library Cataloguing in Publication Data
A catalogue record for this book is available from the British Library.

ISBN 0-7509-1823-3

Typeset in 10/12 Perpetua.
Typesetting and origination by
Sutton Publishing Limited.
Printed in Great Britain by
Ebenezer Baylis, Worcester.

For
Nick Dewey

INTRODUCTION

It is not difficult to picture the scene in homes throughout the land on the evening of 14 May 1940. With ever-worsening news of enemy advances on the continent and the people of Britain fearing the imminent arrival of Germany's massive fighting machine, families huddled around their wireless sets after the BBC's nine o'clock news bulletin to hear an important broadcast made by the Secretary of State for War, Anthony Eden. 'The Government has received countless enquiries from all over the kingdom from men of all ages who wish to do something for the defence of their country,' he intoned. 'Well, now is your opportunity.' By appealing for men aged between seventeen and sixty-five (and not otherwise engaged in military service) to present themselves immediately for enrolment at local police stations, Eden was at that moment publicly giving birth to the Local Defence Volunteers (swiftly to be re-christened the Home Guard).

I imagine there can be few people who, over the past thirty years or so, have not watched at least one episode of the BBC television series *Dad's Army* and for whom the mere mention of the Home Guard would not conjure up visions of the fictional platoon at Walmington-on-Sea. Indeed, for many of us our impressions of the Second World War's 'civilian army' might have been shaped almost entirely by the antics of Captain Mainwaring's platoon, leaving the indelible impression that the Home Guard was well-intentioned but essentially incompetent. However, while the caricature of the typical Home Guard as poorly trained, chaotic, overkeen and a danger to himself and the public may have contained some truth in the early days of the LDV's existence, the effects of training and discipline helped to shape the Home Guard into more of a force to be reckoned with as the war unfolded.

This was not by any means the first occasion in our history when a voluntary civilian force had been assembled at home during a time of international conflict. The tradition goes back to the Napoleonic Wars and beyond. However, the novelty lay in the fact that such a large body of disparate civilians was so swiftly recruited and moulded into a coherent military force, albeit an amateur one.

The Home Guard was 'stood down' at the close of 1944, some months before the end of the war in Europe and, after it had been resurrected (less successfully) for a few years during the 1950s, that was the end of its story. Anyone wishing to read in detail about the Home Guard's history should refer to Norman Longmate's *The Real Dad's Army* (1974) and Professor S.P. Mackenzie's *The Home Guard* (1995), both of which accounts proved invaluable during the preparation of this volume.

I suppose that any family with a Home Guard connection will have its own favourite story, and mine is no exception. My grandfather, a Sergeant-Major in the First World War and a staunch Home Guard in the Second, was about to set off for 'drill practice' at his local pub one evening, while an air-raid was raging in the night skies over his home at Dagenham in Essex. My grandmother remonstrated with him, pleading that he should wait until the 'all-clear' had sounded before leaving the house, but all to no avail. 'Now, my dear, don't worry,' he reassured her. 'If Jerry lands, there'll be thousands of Home Guards all over the country ready to spring into action on the instant.' With that he turned abruptly, toppled off the doorstep and fell headlong into the front garden.

Compiling a book of photographs about the Home Guard is rather like trying to catch grains of sand before they slip through your fingers. Because so many of the men who filled its ranks were already middle-aged or even elderly at the time, sadly a large proportion of former members are no longer with us and – in many cases – their photographs from that tumultuous period have been lost with them. Also, there were stringent restrictions placed on photography during the war. I appealed for Home Guard photographs through almost every local newspaper and BBC radio station in the land, and I am immensely grateful to those many people who scoured their attics and old family albums on my behalf. But even that in itself would not have been sufficient to fill the pages of this volume. Fortunately, I was able to draw on a wonderful collection of Home Guard photographs held at the Imperial War Museum in London, and I must thank John Delaney of the IWM's Photograph Archive for guiding me so patiently through its treasures.

Many of the images that comprise this book are being published for the first time. It is certainly a 'warts-and-all' collection, touching on the one hand upon the humorous and slightly absurd, and on the other upon the heroic and even tragic aspects of the Home Guard's existence. Given that its members were unpaid, perhaps these photographs also serve as a useful reminder that there are occasions in life when a job is worth doing simply for its own sake.

David Carroll
Shieldhill, Dumfriesshire, 1999

Chapter One

In the Beginning

1st Volunteer Battalion, Isle of Wight Regiment Volunteer Training Corps, 'A' Company, 2nd and 3rd Platoons' officers and NCOs, 1919. This photograph was taken at Westwood Football Ground, where the Cowes team still plays. The Volunteer Training Corps (VTC) no doubt used it for exercises as there was a rifle range on the site. Back row, left to right: Cpl E. Lindsay, L/Cpl E.E. Vincent, Cpl T.W. Hudson, Sgt S. Taylor, Sgt Jackman, Cpl J.G. May, L/Cpl G. Wheeler, L/Cpl W. Mahy. Front row: Platoon Sgt F. Warne, 2nd/Lt E. Blachford, Lt H.S. Benzie, Capt. F.W. Boville, 2nd/Lt H.A. Lee, CSM S. Spencer. The VTC was to all intents and purposes the Home Guard of the First World War. It came into existence in 1914, after mounting pressure had been exerted on the Government – not least by such well-known public figures as the writers H.G. Wells and Sir Arthur Conan Doyle – to raise local defence forces, when fears of an invasion grew at home. The VTC was officially dispersed towards the end of 1920. The venue for much of the force's training on the Isle of Wight was the Cowes Drill Hall in Denmark Road. Weekends were usually the time for route marches and manoeuvres, together with musketry practice on the nearby Newtown range.

Right: These men are taking part in a recruiting rally for LDVs held at Poole in Dorset, 8 July 1940. Organised by the local branch of the Citizens' Training Corps, the event was held in the town's Poole Park and attracted local men of all ages – although it seems to be mainly the younger members of the parade who have been captured in this stirring photograph.

LONDON AREA. No..............

Zone ....

LOCAL DEFENCE VOLUNTEERS
CERTIFICATE OF ENROLMENT.

CERTIFIED that ...Frank Henry Bryant......

of ...R. Records Arnside St Walworth SE 17

has been enrolled as a Member of the Local Defence Volunteers.

Dated the 22nd day of June. 1940.

Group H.Q.

....

.... Group Organizer.

A Certificate of Enrolment for the LDV, issued to Frank Bryant on 22 June 1940, in the earliest days of the LDV's existence (and before the name was changed to Home Guard). At the time, Mr Bryant worked in a branch of the War Office based at Arnside Street, Walworth, in south-east London, and – alongside other colleagues who had enrolled as LDVs – his duties included turning out with a rifle whenever the sirens sounded, ostensibly to guard the War Office building and its valuable contents. Mr Bryant recalls that he was issued with an American rifle that arrived still packed in its maker's grease, and that his training consisted merely of one visit to the range at Bisley.

A group of civilians enrolling for duty with the newly formed LDV, 28 May 1940. This photograph, taken at an undisclosed location 'somewhere in England', shows the familiar scene that was being played out at recruitment centres up and down the land in the wake of Anthony Eden's broadcast made two weeks earlier, at a time when invasion by air or sea was expected almost by the hour. Men of all ages – some no more than boys, others approaching their second childhood, and many ignoring the seventeen to sixty-five stipulated age range – flocked to police stations and other hastily organised registration points, in response to the War Minister's plea for those members of the male population who were unable to join the Regular Forces to form a new 'civilian army' at home. Within a day or so of Eden's broadcast nearly a quarter of a million men had enrolled for service. Six weeks later, at the end of June, the number had grown to almost one and a half million, far outstripping the War Office's expectations. However, such an unexpected and overwhelmingly enthusiastic response soon caused unforeseen problems. The task of enrolling so many men in such a short space of time proved to be an administrative nightmare, simply because no framework of bureaucracy had been established for the LDV in its earliest, haphazard days. The force had been brought into existence virtually within forty-eight hours of the haziest plans for its formation being sketched out in a series of hastily convened meetings at the War Office. As a result, eager recruits would often turn up to 'sign on', only to discover that the enrolment officer had run out of official application forms. (Backs of envelopes and other odd slips of paper were routinely used as a substitute.) The authorities simply could not keep pace with the demand. Later, organising such a large and unwieldy body of men into the platoons, companies and battalions which comprised the force that was subsequently re-christened the Home Guard proved to be a task of daunting proportions.

Many factories organised their own units of LDVs (unkindly dubbed the 'Look, Duck and Vanish Brigade' by comedians), just like the group of employees seen here at Evershed & Vignoles in Chiswick, west London, pictured during their first parade on Sunday 7 July 1940. These men went on to form part of the 7th County of London Battalion Home Guard. Note the array of broom handles to compensate for the lack of rifles! Back row, left to right: S.A. Brackley, A.J. Littlefield, G. Taylor, A.E. Willcock, P. Roney, S.G. Wallis, J.W. Greenhough, R.W. Neale, T.E. Kenny, H.R. Halling, L.H. Smart. Front row: W.A. Gregory, F.A. Smith, C.H. Patterson, E. Payton, H. Ruggles, G.E. Lawson, J.E. Strong, J.A. King, A.E. Piper, G.A. Eveleigh, B. Higginbotham.

LDVs on parade in Montpellier Gardens, Cheltenham, Gloucestershire, summer 1940. This group of men was soon absorbed into the 1st Gloucestershire Battalion Home Guard, whose area embraced Cheltenham, Winchcombe, Dumbleton and Tewkesbury. Of course, there were no uniforms at first and LDV armbands (as worn by the men here) were provided – in this case – with the enthusiastic assistance of the Red Cross, WVS, British Legion and students of Cheltenham Art School. Despite a chronic national shortage of weapons throughout LDV units, this group appears to be well provided with rifles as there is not a broom handle in sight!

In the fullness of time there was hardly a square yard of the country not under nocturnal observation by one Home Guard unit or another. It was a state of affairs well illustrated by this early and poignant photograph of two elderly LDVs (and their dog), keeping an armed watch in the gathering dusk for German parachutists over a lonely stretch of the South Downs in Sussex, May 1940. Being so near the south coast the area was considered particularly vulnerable to enemy landings.

Mr R. Holland-Martin, Chairman of the Southern Railway Company, is setting an example here to the Southern Railway's workforce by enrolling as 'SR Home Guard No. 1' in the early summer of 1940. The Southern Railway Home Guard was specially authorised by the War Office, and a total of 35,000 employees enrolled for service during the course of the war. The primary aim, of course, was to protect the Southern Railway system from enemy attack.

LDVs (left to right: Will Harrison, Pud Walker, George Key and Gerry McCallum) are pictured here during look-out duty on the village church tower in Aslackby, south of Sleaford, summer 1940. This vantage point afforded the men a commanding view over the flat Lincolnshire Fens which lay spread out below them. Any Germans landing by parachute in the area would have been spotted immediately. In that event, the men were instructed to run to the local post office and ask the postmaster to telephone LDV headquarters for assistance. (In the meantime, no doubt, our helpful enemy parachutist would loiter nearby awaiting capture!) Most members of the platoon – which in due course comprised part of 'D' Company, 4th Kesteven Battalion Home Guard, based at nearby Bourne – worked on the land, but the unit also included a couple of blacksmiths and Sgt Jack Hemphrey, the landlord of the local Red Lion pub. The men in this photograph are still sporting LDV armbands, which were the only means of distinguishing members of the new 'civilian army' until the piecemeal issue of uniforms took place over the ensuing months.

There were no sophisticated alarm systems available to call out LDV units in the event of an emergency. The ringing of church bells was to be the signal everywhere that an invasion had occurred. However, one English village adapted this ship's bell for the purpose. The bell, it appears, had earlier served its time on a vessel called the City of New York sailing out of Liverpool. The photograph was taken on 12 August 1940, by which time the LDV had officially become known as the Home Guard.

CHAPTER TWO

LINE-UPS

Members of the Tavistock Home Guard, Devon, 1941/2. Among those identified here are, back row, left to right: Messrs Grigg, McNicholl, Parnell, Lake, Rice, Hoare, Brooks, Wilcocks. Middle row: Messrs Merrett, Burrows, Sussex, Price, Abel, Cundy. Front row: Messrs Dawe, Everson, Gill, Greaves, Verran, Johnson, Harvey, Hoare, Symons, Wilton, Knott, Waterfield.

The Wangford Platoon of the 4th Suffolk Battalion Home Guard, 1943. Back row, left to right: 'Wimp' Smith, 'Spider' Woolnaugh, H. Gant, Stanley Wright, 'Hub' Walton, C. Saunders, Dick Nelson, J. Lark, Harry Lewis, P. Gissing. Middle row: P. Rumbelow, A. Stockdale, F. Bullard, G. Reynolds, H. Bacon, Alex Hill, 'Fire' Keable, W. Walker, Sydney Fiske. Front row: G. Frezzer, George Lytton, H. Peck, Capt. Noel, Capt. Paisley, Major Chenery, CSM King, Bertie Walker, 'Rollie' Keable, L. Whyte. One former member of this platoon at Wangford (a village near Southwold), recalls that the Home Guard was on duty every night outside the local police station. Sunday mornings were devoted to parading and bayonet drill, '. . . and the next stop the pub'.

The 2nd County of London (Victoria, Chelsea, Kensington) Battalion Home Guard photographed in the forecourt of Wellington Barracks, Birdcage Walk, 13 May 1944, prior to mounting the King's Guard at nearby Buckingham Palace. It was just one of many events held in the capital and around the country to mark the Home Guard's fourth anniversary. Back row, left to right: M. Prior, A. Rookley, J. Stovold, W.H. Page, H. Smith, A. Wightman, F. Capes, D. Halstead, A. Mayer, L. Bruce. Third row: J. Killingback, H. Anthony, R. Boxter, D. Porteus, K. Drew, C. Metcalfe, C. Alcock, F. Craft, F. Newton, D. Murch, R. Ellis. Second row: Sgt B. Hoey, W. Locke, D. Avery, C. West, H. Shafe, R. Hudson, D. Heatlie, R. Drabble, B. Hurrell, F. Gyford, R. Stafford, G.L. Page, L. Greaves, J. Hodgson, C. Copp, J.V. Stevenson. Front row: B. Okill, Sgt P. McCormack, D/Sgt J. Barker, Lt T. Clarke, CSM W. Dalton, Capt. J. Durran, Capt. & Adjutant D. Fenton Smith, Lt F. South, Sgt J. Cameron, Sgt L. Stevens, Cpl J. Hughes.

The men of Heathfield Home Guard, near Taunton, Somerset. Back row, left to right: Victor Henry Babb, Ernest William Lock, Clement Charles Matthews, Richard John Smith, George William Swain, Gordon Summers. Front row: Leslie Cornish, John Bodger, Charles John Thomson, Thomas William Bodger, Colin George Thomson. The platoon (most of whose members were agricultural workers) was drilled on the front lawn of Heathfield Manor Farm. A local eye-witness to these proceedings claims that some of the men experienced difficulty at first in telling right from left, thereby causing mild amusement in the village on training nights.

The Frampton Mansell Home Guard Platoon near Stroud, Gloucestershire. Standing, left to right: F. Musty, A. Roberts, H. Gardiner, K. Musty, H.G. Smith, L. Workman, -?-, -?-, A. Jones, W. Roberts. Front row: F. Ash, W. Jones, J. Musty, P. Baxter, S. Perry, -?-, T. Gardiner. A former member of this rural unit recalls that every night two men from the platoon were detailed to guard the southern entrance of the railway tunnel at Sapperton. The men – armed with a rifle and, by all accounts, a pitchfork – would position themselves approximately 100 yards inside the tunnel's entrance, so that they could see the approach of any enemy without being spotted themselves.

The Blunsdon Home Guard Platoon near Swindon, Wiltshire. Back row, left to right: W. Kemble, E. Walsh, W. Wiltshire, R. Kemble, J. Kemble, J. Cole, H. Mills, P. Mills, W. Stroud. Fourth row: E. Beazley, I. Wiltshire, F. Mulcock, T. Card, H. Kemble, Mr Vines, A. Percival, C. Kemble, F. Wilkins, F. Curtis. Third row: B. Card, R. Mulcock, H. Cole, H. Painter, B. Nicholls, Mr Skinner, E. Adams, A. Drew, J. Jackson, J. Pearce, F. Brunsdon, A. New. Second row: A. Staples, W. Mulcock, G. Wiltshire, T. Adams, T. Green, Major Archer, S. Maundrell, Mr King, W. Wiltshire, J. Adams, Mr Groves. Front row: P. Stroud, S. Marshall, R. Wiltshire, E. Stroud, Mr Parry, T. Sandle, G. Agamber, J. Mulcock.

Members of the Strangford Home Guard, County Down, Northern Ireland. Back row, left to right: A. Sage, J.J. Shields, R. Allen, W. Jackson, H. Quayle, A. Hinds. Middle row: J. Allen, A. Matthews, J. Grey, J. Swail, H. Torney, G. Johnson, Wm Orr, J. McIlheron. Front row: T. Henderson, J. Coates, G. Quayle, E. Pinkerton, P. Beattie, G. Jackson, R. Sullivan. Ulster's equivalent of the Home Guard was raised in late May 1940, soon after the formation of the LDV, and it was linked with the police force – the Royal Ulster Constabulary – rather than being under military control, as was the case elsewhere in the United Kingdom.

The Hopesay Home Guard Platoon near Craven Arms, Shropshire. Back row, left to right: Eddie Cadwallader, -?-, Walter Hotchkiss, Tom Gwilliam, Kenny Habershon, Lewis Payne, Arthur Payne, Bill Burgoyne. Front row: Ernie Bason, Mr Evans, E.B. Lloyd, Stan Whittingham, Charlie Bason, George Price, Arthur Jukes, Harry Evans (jnr), Bill Bason (snr), Harry Evans (snr), Bill Payne, Arthur Sincup (Officer in Charge of the platoon). The lady standing to the left of the group is Miss Blandford, and the house in the background can still be seen in Hopesay – a village south of the Long Mynd.

The Warter Home Guard Platoon near Pocklington, in the former East Riding of Yorkshire, 1942/3. Most of the men pictured here were employed on the Warter Priory Estate as farmworkers, gamekeepers and so on. The Commanding Officer was Estate Manager Mr R.H. Campbell (front row, centre). Former platoon member Mr F.C. Patrick (who provided this photograph) recalls that, during the unit's early days, the men had no uniforms or weapons and drilled with broom handles (a very familiar story!) A few men – for example the gamekeepers – did possess double-barrelled shotguns. Eventually, however, uniforms and Lee Enfield rifles arrived, and the platoon drilled, did firing practice, and erected road blocks, and undertook many a dawn patrol up on the Yorkshire Wolds.

Members of the Warninglid Home Guard Platoon, between Horsham and Haywards Heath in Sussex. Back row, left to right: Ron Lewrey, Arthur Goatcher, Benny Salisbury, George Privett, Fred Upton. Front row: Jim Newnham, Tom Newnham, Lt Walter Munn, Sgt Pat O'Shea, Cpl Bill Stephens. The men are pictured here standing outside Warninglid's village hall, which was the platoon's headquarters.

The men of Sanday Home Guard were drawn from and served one of the most northerly islands in the Orkney archipelago. (Owing to the occasional repetition of names, something that is inevitable in a small community, brief addresses are given here where possible to help with identification.) Back row, left to right: William Skea (North Myre), Mr Thomson, David Towrie (Clickimin), John Tulloch (Upperhouse Ortie), Peter Fotheringhame (Rusness), Peter Harcus (Lealand), John Muir (Backaskaill), Thomas Cursiter (Stove), William Skea (Elsness), James Skea, James Tulloch (Braehower), Thomas Moodie, Fraser Horne (Warsetter), Malcolm Manson, William Sinclair (Elsness). Third row: Thomas Garrioch (Neigarth), Oliver Meil (Tressness), William Tulloch (Upperhouse Ortie), James Skea (East Langamay), Donald Sinclair (Elsness), Robert Muir (Backaskaill), James Skea (North Myre), James O. Alexander (Thorness), John Swanney (North Hower), Peter Gray (Newark), Billy Skea (Elsness), George Hay (Waterhall), William Dearness (Myrtlelane), William Dearness (Mid Breckan), John Williamson (Hammerbrake), William Muir (Kettletoft), John Thomson (Ortie). Second row: Andrew Williamson (Hammerbrake), George Learmouth (Little Isgarth), John Bews (Warsetter), John Drever (Gresmay), Andrew Skea (Rusness), John Tulloch (Kettletoft), William Moodie, Rev. Alexander Ralston, James Baillie, Walter Garrioch (Odinsgarth), David Rousay (Fieldquoy), William Ward (Scar), William Rendall, William Tulloch, James Cooper (Little Savilgreen), David Marwick (Coo), David King (Hermisgarth). Front row: Walter Mainland (Laminess Southend), Andrew Sinclair (Mid Myre), Andrew Thomson (Stove), John Dearness (Quoylealand), James Sinclair (Kettletoft), Lionel Munro, John Allan (Bressigarth), William Muir (Bridgend), David Muir (Savilgreen), James Muir (Ayre), William Towrie (Clickimin), William Williamson (Hammerbrake), Harry Scott (Stumpo).

Members of the Kendal Home Guard Platoon in Westmorland pictured outside the town's Drill Hall, 1940. Those identified here are as follows. Back row: Jim Bell, Teddy Jordan. Fourth row: John Wood, Jack Summers, Ray Fleetwood. Third row: Jack Troughton, Fred Bowker, Brian Coulter. Second row: Jack Robinson (Commanding Officer), Bill Leather, Jumbo Dawson. Front row: Arnold Hodgson, Ernie Coward, Jim Donohue. A former member of the platoon recalls that, in addition to 'square bashing' and weapon training, the men undertook nightly duty at the local police station. Weekends were devoted to exercises on a nearby fellside, when the platoon was able to use live ammunition – including real hand grenades instead of paper bags filled with flour.

No. 5 Platoon (Blackford) 'A' Company of the 5th Perthshire Battalion Home Guard. This photograph was taken in 1941/2, shortly after the platoon had been issued with uniforms and rifles. Most of the men seen here were farmers or farmworkers in reserved occupations. The platoon met once a week for drill in Blackford's Free Church Hall and did shooting practice at Comrie. The battalion, under the command of Major Stirling, drew members from an area that included Blackford, Braco, Comrie and Dunblane. Local farmer George Sharp, seated in the front row wearing civilian clothing, organised the recruitment of Blackford's Volunteer Training Corps during the First World War.

No. 1 Platoon, No. 1 Company of the 11th Norfolk Battalion Home Guard was based at Gorleston near Great Yarmouth. Captain Connors is seated in the centre of the front row, flanked by Pl. Sgt P. Webb (left) and Billy Woods (right). Names of some other platoon members pictured here are Graves, Lockwood, Mason, Brundish, Ditcham, Crowther, Barnes, Burrall, Scott, Durrant, Calthorpe, Leggett and Symonds. Apparently, the platoon's HQ was an empty requisitioned house in Poplar Avenue, although one former member of the unit recalls that meetings and parades were actually held at Church Road School and at a house on Gorleston cliffs. Some manoeuvres and exercises were carried out at Fellowes Shipyard, Southtown, and shooting practice was undertaken at Herringfleet.

Members of the Dingwall Home Guard Platoon, Ross-shire, 1940/1. Those identified here are, back row: D. Mackenzie, J. Matheson, N. Watt. Middle row: A. Harrower, T. Sinclair, N. Armstrong, A. Shanks, A. MacFarlane, A. Arnot, D. Mackenzie, S. Ross. Front row: A MacLennen, Lt Thomson, D. Fanning, D. MacBeath, J. Reid.

The assembled ranks of 'B' Company, 11th Cornwall (Newquay) Battalion Home Guard ('the Choughs'), photographed in 1944 on the town's golf course. Back row, left to right: ? Prout, L. Emmett, H. Goudge, D. Todman, C. Palmer, D. Craddock, -?-, J. Bennett, N. Derrick, M. Chegwidden, J. Irish, P. Bennett, G. Hawke, -?-, ? Thomas, R. Owen. Sixth row: A. Old, ? Burt, A. Haris, A. Barrett, J. Willis, -?-, J. Trethewey, ? Williams, -?-, -?-, -?-, K. Mitchelmore, T. Hooper, W. Jacka, -?-, -?-. Fifth row: V. Pascoe, W. Tamblyn, R. Garlick, L. Richards, E. Barber, H. Mathews, F. Fallis, -?-, J. Gilbert, A. Nott, ? Irish, D. Docking. Fourth row: ? Stephens, J. Bennett, M. Chudleigh, W. Jago, -?-, A. Williams, -?-, S.E. Harris, -?-, -?-, A. Rawle, ? Stevens, D. Morris, ? Magor, G. Flamank, H. Gwynn, K. Cave. Third row: -?-, E. Goudge, C. Docking, W. Helliwell, G. Paull, F. Maynard, -?-, W. Cook, -?-, S. Bernard, G. Rawlings, L. Kent, ? Endean. Second row: R. Whyman, C. Sloggett, ? Harris, J. Littlechild, B. Burt, L. Clemens, R. Williams, W. Gilbert, R. Harris, C. Ruse, -?-, L. Snell, C. Isaacs, H. Griggs, A. Hicks, T. Curry, H. Herman, B. Craddock, L. Tonkin, W. Stephens, A. Searle, S. Long. Front row: S. Langmaid, M. Bennett, W. Slater, W. Kerridge, W. Owen, K. Taylor, E.H. Trembath, R.E. Harris, W. Moyse.

The Aslackby Platoon, 'D' Company, 4th Kesteven Battalion Home Guard, near Sleaford in Lincolnshire. Back row, left to right: Sam Harvey, Kelly Williamson, Sunny Cook, Lewis Harrison, Vic Bates, Bob Pick, Arthur Walker, Bill Reynolds, Don Bates, Will Harrison, Gerry McCallum. Middle row: Fred Christian, Ray Stanton, Chris Sharpe, Frank Andrews, Bill Key, Ron Stanton, Dossy Wells. Front row: Jack Hemphrey, C. Martin, Bill Christian, Charlie Christian.

No. 1 Platoon, 'D' Company, 1st Ayrshire Battalion Home Guard, 1942. Back row, left to right: Ptes Norman Whitehead, Norman Carline, Jack Hargreaves, Jock Barnes, Stan Comben, Robert Downey, Jack White. Middle row: Ptes Harry McGinty, Bill Pritchard, Bill Landers, Don McFarlane, -?-, Hugh McNair, Jack Walker, Eric Barnes, Bert Simpson. Front row: L/Cpl Freedman, L/Cpl Frank Pye, Cpl Dennis Flann, Sgt E. Keynes, Lt Felix Apthorpe, 2nd Lt Norman Coggs, S/Sgt Nevil Thurgood, Sgt Gus Gilbert, Cpl John Hughes, L/Cpl Jim Cartland.

Members of No. 22 Platoon, 'F' company, 4th Herefordshire Battalion Home Guard. Back row, left to right: R.W. Lawrence, G. Handley, G. Hicks, W.H. Stinton, A. Mills, J. Stinton, I.J. Humphries. Third row: W. Montague, J.H. Black, G. Reynolds, G. Hughes, H. Peake, G. Holder, H. Bayliss, F. Montague. Second row: R. Langford, J.R. Lewis, W. Portman, T. Skyrme, L/Cpl G.J. Price, A.C. Hart, R. Davies, D. Hamer, F. Evans. Front row: L/Cpl R. Eacock, L/Cpl S. Baugh, Sgt G. Haines, Coy QM Lt G.S. Lawrence, Coy Cmdr Major J.A. Hollis, Pl. Cmdr Capt. P.B. Compton, Sgt A.J. Powell, Cpl R.G. Jones, L/Cpl P.H. Aiderton. This photograph, dating from 1943 or 1944, was taken in the grounds of the Garnons estate at Byford, about 2 miles from Staunton-on-Wye.

No. 1 Platoon, 'C' Company, 5th London Battalion Home Guard (The King's Royal Rifle Corps), 1944. Based in St John's Wood, members of the unit were trained as sharp shooters. Those identified here are, seated: Cpl Gluxsten, Sgt Warner, Lt Hoad, Cpl Hedley. Standing: Messrs Stier, Worricker, Goldsmith, Morris, Beauman, Gelber, Stalker, Salmeir, Hinrichsen, Ilys. Klaus Hinrichsen (the tallest person in the back row) was a German refugee, recently released from internment on the Isle of Man.

Kempsford Platoon, 3rd Gloucestershire (Cirencester) Battalion Home Guard, July 1943. Back row, left to right: K. Merritt, F. Burry, F. Watkins, V. Packer, J. Spackman, C. Waite, F. Couling, W. James. Third row: S. Mullcock, W. Higgs, H. Jones, C. Hobbs, B. Couling, W. Couling, J. King, G. Cox, S. Hicks, W. Holbrook, N. Cook. Second row: T. Smith, A. Higgs, F. Wakefield, W. Kelly, W. Blakey, F. Bullock, C. King, A. Arkell, L. Chamberlain, F. Ockwell, G. Butler. Front row: R. Ockwell, A. Bradley, A. Nicholls, C. Kent, G. Goodman, Major Northern, Capt. Clark, the Revd Mr Caton (and Roger), J. Coton, Col. Lawrence (and Blaze), J. Ockwell, F. Carpenter, W. Woods, I. Cleaver.

Longparish Home Guard Platoon, near Andover, Hampshire. Among those pictured outside Upper Mill in the village are the following. Back row, left to right: Harry Weeks, Ginger Smith, Gordon Howell, Sgt Juff, George Howell. Front row: Bill Tonge, Will Winton, Eddy Kimber, Fred Dewey, Geoff Cook, Cecil Williams. Here, as elsewhere throughout the country, the platoon comprised men of all ages, ranging from boys hardly out of school to veterans of the First World War and even earlier conflicts. It was this enormous diversity of age and experience within each unit that characterised the Home Guard everywhere.

Members of the 203rd GHQ Reserve Home Guard pictured at Bath, *c.* 1941. Back row, left to right: Pte E. Dwane, Pte A.P. James, Pte N.J. James, Pte W.W. Curry, Pte J. Blair, Pte S.R.G. Saunter. Pte L.M. Pusey, Pte H.D. Rees BEM, Pte W.F.E. Emmerson. Third row: Pte H. Masters, Pte C.J. Gates, L/Cpl R.A. Partridge, Pte S.L. Baldery, Pte F.N. Jermy, Pte H. Banham, Pte R.A.D. Heward, Pte A.P. Morgan, Pte P.F. Carter, Pte T.F. Pope, L/Cpl R.N. Reeds. Second row: Pte R.M.B. Judson, L/Cpl S.F. Phillips, Pte E. White, Sgt E.A. Sterne, Sgt N.W.S. Baker BEM, Sgt N.E. Shephard, L/Cpl E. Roscorla, Pte N. Armstrong, Pte J. O'B. Canavan. Front row: Sgt D.F. Stevenson, 2nd/Lt G.R.M. Hutchings, Capt. L.A. Aves, Lt J.G. Spearman, 2nd/Lt I. McG. Phillips BEM, Sgt R.W. Bennet. This is a rare photograph of the men attached to the Home Guard's so-called 'secret army', an organisation whose existence was only revealed thirty years ago when the relevant Cabinet Papers were released, but whose activities remained until even more recently one of the war's best-kept secrets. Hand-picked members of the Home Guard were invited to undergo special training to become, in effect, an élite guerrilla force; a body kept wholly secret not only from the public at large but also within the Home Guard itself. Although the men wore Home Guard uniforms, they did not attend parades or carry out normal duties. Around three thousand men were trained to form these Auxiliary Units, which were set up in the coastal counties around Britain. The training centre for this 'British Resistance' was established at Coleshill Manor near Swindon where, during intensive weekend courses, members drawn from Auxiliary Units throughout the country would be versed in the art of sabotage. Attached to GHQ Home Forces, the 'secret army' was eventually formed into special battalions unconnected to those of the ordinary Home Guard. Underground hideaways on the North Yorkshire Moors, concealed chambers below the South Downs and submerged bunkers in the Mendip Hills all give some flavour of how the Home Guard's 'secret army' operated.

CHAPTER THREE

RAILWAY & WATERBORNE UNITS

During the war Britain was served by a network of main and branch railway lines extending over 20,000 miles, every yard of which was patrolled by members of the Home Guard. This photograph, taken on a stretch of track in suburban north London at the beginning of July 1940, shows four Local Defence Volunteers from Palmers Green and Winchmore Hill stations. They were all London & North-East Railway employees who had been recruited as members of that company's own Home Guard force.

This atmospheric photograph, possibly designed as a publicity shot to aid recruitment, shows a member of a railway Home Guard unit on duty as a train steams out of a London terminus in the early morning of 30 July 1940. The chap seen here was luckier than most of his colleagues. He had acquired a bayonet, a tin helmet and a reasonably well-fitting uniform, all within a week or so of the LDV being reinvented as the Home Guard (at the insistence of Prime Minister Winston Churchill).

It was essential, of course, that Britain's entire railway system – its tracks, bridges, stations, signal-boxes and rolling-stock – should be fully protected from any damage or disruption that might be inflicted by German parachutists or through other enemy action. As a result, each of the railway companies that operated the network in those pre-nationalisation days had swiftly formed its own squads of Local Defence Volunteers, within just days or weeks of the War Minister's call for a 'civilian army'. Railway company bosses had been quick to see the wisdom of recruiting their own employees as Railway Home Guards and, reflecting the famous 'wartime spirit' that existed throughout the country, a new sense of pulling together permeated the workforce. Here, a motley crew drawn from Southern Railway's hotel staff (above), together with a group of Southern Railway porters (below), are being trained in the handling and use of rifles by soldiers from the Regular Army. The men are pictured on the roof of a London station in early June 1940.

At the beginning of August 1940, when this photograph was taken, it was estimated that well in excess of 100,000 railway employees throughout the country were already playing an active part in one or other of the railways' own Home Guard units. The two men pictured here, prior to taking up their positions for a spell of night guard duty, were members of the London Midland & Scottish Railway Home Guard based at Manchester Central station. They are both still wearing LDV armbands, although the force had by then been renamed the Home Guard.

Glastonbury railway station Home Guard, Somerset, 1941/2. The station lay on the old Somerset and Dorset line (known as the 'slow and dirty' or the 'swift and delightful', depending on your point of view). A former member of the unit recalls that, at the time this photograph was taken, the platoon was equipped with 'a Lewis machine-gun that was always jamming; a Blacker Bombard (or Spigot Mortar) made from bits of steel and of uncertain accuracy; an American Tommy gun with, later on, a few Sten guns and some old Canadian Ross rifles. To sum up,' he concluded, 'if the Germans had landed we would all have been "blown away" forthwith!' Sgt Rodd is pictured fourth from the right in the front row.

The Southern Railway Home Guard was divided into six battalions, each of which was attached to a county regiment. Here, a party from the 2nd Southern Railway (25th Sussex) Battalion Home Guard is undergoing instruction in the use of the Blacker Bombard (or Spigot Mortar), closely watched by Southern Railway's General Manager and his entourage. This photograph was probably taken at Gomshall, between Guildford and Dorking in Surrey, where a training centre for the entire Southern Railway Home Guard was set up on land adjoining the station. Similar centres were also created at Brockenhurst in the New Forest and at Chatham in Kent.

Southern Railway's Bricklayer's Arms Goods Depot, a stone's-throw from the Old Kent Road in south-east London, had the distinction of forming the country's first railway Home Guard Band, whose members can be seen marching and playing in this photograph. The band was formed in early 1941, and the intruments were purchased through a voluntary subscription of 1*d* a week paid by members of 'C' Company, 6th Southern Railway (36th County of London) Battalion Home Guard.

A great deal of emphasis was placed on anti-aircraft training in the Southern Railway Home Guard, and elsewhere throughout Britain's railway network, because enemy reprisals were feared at home in response to allied attacks on locomotive depots in Europe. In an effort to counteract this threat seventeen units, known as Home Guard Independent Light Anti-Aircraft Troops, were formed by the various battalions throughout the Southern Railway system. Guns were mounted in positions where they could be manned within a few seconds, to be operated both at night and also during periods of possible daylight raids. This photograph, taken at Exmouth Junction Depot in Devon on 27 March 1944, shows Southern Railway Home Guards, left to right, Gnr J. Bezzant, Sgt F. Western (Detachment Commander), Gnr W. Brook (Loader & Firer), Gnr W. Ware. They were all members of Troop K LAA, 5th Southern Railway (22nd Devon) Battalion Home Guard. The manning of anti-aircraft batteries by Home Guard personnel around the country called – as this photograph demonstrates – for a degree of expertise and discipline that is sometimes at odds with the public perception of Britain's wartime 'civilian army'. Also, tales of discord between the Regular Army and Home Guard crop up occasionally. Whatever may be the truth or otherwise of these stories, the two forces worked harmoniously together on anti-aircraft sites, with the part-time amateurs and full-time soldiers operating alongside each other as closely knit teams.

A Great Western Railway Home Guard platoon, photographed at Cheltenham, Gloucestershire, in 1944. Initially the men trained at the spa town's Drill Hall but permission was eventually sought and obtained to use the Ladies' College playing field for the purpose. In the course of its history, the Great Western Railway Home Guard unit at Cheltenham provided Guards of Honour for Queen Mary and the Duchess of Gloucester. Also, two special GWR parades were held, including one at Gloucester in 1943. The final GWR parade took place at Weston-super-Mare, when five railway divisions were gathered together. Men from as far apart as London and Penzance attended the occasion.

The Ladywood Motor Patrol boat, manned by its small crew of armed Home Guards, sets out on observation duty along the canal system in the Ladywood district of Birmingham, 19 August 1940. Among the various waterborne Home Guard units that sprang up around the country at the time, this was perhaps one of the least trumpeted. It must be said that the vessel is not a prepossessing sight, seemingly incapable of much speed and – on the evidence of this photograph – less well equipped than other similar units. Nevertheless, these men are performing a valuable function at some possible risk to themselves, in the heart of what was then one of England's great industrial cities.

Members of the Upper Thames Patrol gather for a conference with 'stretch-commander' Guy W. Bridgewater (seated) before setting out on duty, 22 July 1940. Within only a few days of Anthony Eden's call for the formation of a 'civilian army' Sir Ralph Glyn, Tory Member of Parliament for Abingdon, asked the War Minister for permission to establish a waterborne unit of Local Defence Volunteers along the upper reaches of the River Thames. He was swiftly granted his request and the Upper Thames Patrol was formed. Men with experience of handling boats and a knowledge of the river were particularly welcome. As a result, many an old sailor was given the opportunity to revive his nautical skills.

Crew members of an Upper Thames Patrol motor launch are pictured here during a spell of duty on the river, July 1940. The various units protected that part of the Thames running between Lechlade in Gloucestershire and Teddington in Middlesex. The patrols were divided into 16 mile stretches (each presided over by a 'stretch-commander'), and crews maintained a watch both day and night. Riverside pumping stations, bridges, locks and weirs were all deemed at risk from enemy action. In this photograph, dating from LDV days, the men are sporting vaguely naval dress. Later, this was swapped for the ordinary Home Guard uniform.

The War Office decided from the outset that women should be barred from enrolling as Local Defence Volunteers, and it was not until 1943 that they were admitted into the Home Guard as Auxiliaries. (Even then they were not allowed to carry weapons, and an identity badge or armlet was all that served as a uniform.) However, as this photograph taken in 1940 demonstrates, some women had already been working as 'unofficial' Auxiliaries for years. This young lady, at the wheel of an Upper Thames Patrol motor launch, divided her time between secretarial duties ashore and daylight patrols on the river.

Is this simply a group of carefree holiday-makers enjoying a day-trip on the River Thames, or could they possibly be a bunch of enemy agents intent on some act of sabotage? During the summer of 1940, when this photograph was taken, appearances could be deceptive and fears that an active Fifth Column was at work in Britain had reached their height. To ensure that they are as innocent as they seem, a member of the Upper Thames Patrol checks this smiling quartet's identity papers before allowing them to resume their journey.

The Trent River Patrol sprang into action barely a month after the formation of the LDV, and mounted a dusk to dawn surveillance along the River Trent from Sawley (south of Nottingham) through to the Humber estuary. As obvious natural barriers, substantial waterways such as the Trent would have provided useful opportunities to mount an effective defence against invaders. Here, the *Cygnet* sets out on patrol along a stretch of the river with an armed and vigilant crew of Home Guards, 19 September 1940.

A speedy fighter vessel belonging to the Trent River Patrol Home Guard is pictured here during a spell of duty on 12 April 1943. Note the camouflaged cabin and manned machine-gun position on the stern. A large number of the men comprising this unit were either local boat owners or had some other close connection with the river. Sadly, the Trent River Patrol suffered a number of fatalities among its members. Two men were accidentally shot during gun practice and another couple were drowned while on duty.

Armed members of the Trent River Patrol are seen here demonstrating how they would deal with a group of invading Germans should the enemy attempt to cross the river, 22 September 1940. During the course of this exercise, carried out on the Trent near Nottingham, one section of the Home Guard acted as would-be invaders while this trio occupied an observation post close by the river to await possible enemy sightings.

Among the Trent River Patrol's many and varied duties, one of the most vital would have been to maintain communication on either side of the river in the event of enemy landings. In this photograph two signallers from the unit are seen hauling telephone lines across the Trent after contacting the opposite bank by rocket line, 11 April 1943. The Trent River Patrol Home Guard developed into a highly efficient waterborne organisation with over 100 miles of river to protect.

Members of the waterborne section of the 9th Westmorland Battalion Home Guard landing at Millerground on Windermere (above), and Pilot H. Pattinson and Gnr R. Gilbey patrolling the lake during exercises in one of the unit's vessels (below). The Windermere waterborne Home Guard comprised two groups. One was based at the old Drill Hall in Windermere and the other at Borwick's boatyard in nearby Bowness. Under the command of Major Cooper-Pattinson, the unit's job was to patrol the waters of the lake itself (over 10 miles in length) from Waterhead in the north to Lakeside in the south. Among the vessels employed were *Josaphine*, *Winander* and *Merlin*, each equipped with a mounting for a Vickers machine-gun. According to a former member of the unit, the Windermere waterborne Home Guard comprised over one hundred men at its height, although numbers were seriously depleted after 1943, when many of its younger members were called up into the Regular Services. The lake had been protected by one of the Army's own inland waterways sections prior to the formation of the Windermere waterborne Home Guard.

Chapter Four

Other Unusual Units

This photograph of the 'Fast Cycle' Home Guard Platoon from Cheltenham, Gloucestershire, taken in 1941, gives a whole new meaning to the comedy actor Jack Warner's famous catchphrase of the time, 'Mind my bike'. Left to right: Sgt Gladden, Cpl Chapman, Bill Smith, Mr Hackett, Mr Barogrove, Frank Bryant, Roy Williams, George Bream, Mr Webley, Bill Brittam. Former platoon member Frank Bryant recalls that the unit was trained by a Coldstream Guards captain who led the way on his motorcycle. Riding behind furiously on their push-bikes, the men attempted to keep up with him as they travelled along the winding and undulating roads and lanes of Gloucestershire, negotiating hedgerows, ditches, fences and more than one very muddy field in the process. Once fully trained, however, the platoon's main function was to intercept any Germans who may have dropped by parachute in the surrounding area and, in Mr Bryant's words, 'make a thorough nuisance of ourselves until the real Army troops arrived. We thought it was a real suicide job!' Local inhabitants must surely have wondered at the time, when encountering this unlikely platoon careering along at full pelt, what possible relevance a dozen or so men on bicycles (and not all of the riders in the first flush of youth) could possibly have borne to the rigours of the 'real' war that faced the population every day.

The Home Guard on Dartmoor, near Chagford, 30 July 1940. Members of the Mid-Devon Hunt used their own horses in connection with their Home Guard duties, and this photograph taken below Middle Tor shows them forming up before going to their various posts on the moor. Covering over 300 square miles Dartmoor, with its dense woodlands, secluded combes and rugged terrain, would have been an ideal spot for enemy parachute landings. On the debit side, however, the area's impenetrable mists and dangerous swamps might well have caused some problems for any invaders unfamiliar with the geography of the place.

The heights of Exmoor were also patrolled nightly by members of the Home Guard on horseback (and some on bicycles, apparently). Here, in a photograph dating from June 1940, a group of LDVs, all of them having enrolled for service under Mr S.L. Hancock, Master of the Devon and Somerset Stag Hounds, can be seen on a flank of Malmsmead Hill near Oare, in the heart of 'Lorna Doone country'. Of course, mounted Home Guards drawn from the hunting fraternity were of inestimable value in remote moorland regions of this kind, where they were closely acquainted with every square inch of the terrain.

As these two photographs demonstrate, Home Guards on horseback were by no means confined to the country's wild and inaccessible regions. Watched by a small but inquisitive group of bystanders, the Maidenhead Mounted Home Guard (above) is seen during its first outing through the streets of this sedate Berkshire town, 17 September 1940. As if to emphasise the gulf between the resources available to the Home Guard and those enjoyed by the Regular Army, the horsemen are passed by another means of defence, a Bren gun carrier. Below, members of the Maidenhead Mounted Home Guard are engaged in a full-blooded charge on the outskirts of the town, in a scene – it must be said – that is more reminiscent of a horse-racing event than of one bearing any close relation to the needs of serious warfare. Comprising members of the Garth Hunt, farmers and jockeys, it was thought that this mounted Berkshire unit of the Home Guard might prove particularly useful if local roads were sufficiently damaged to prevent the flow of ordinary traffic.

Sgt Steven Varre (right), an instructor in rough riding during the First World War, is pictured here giving Mr F.E. Andrews a few hints on shooting from the saddle, 8 August 1940. Mr Andrews (still wearing an LDV armband although he was by now a Home Guard) belonged to another mounted unit which, in this instance, patrolled the remote North Yorkshire moors. The majority of members were farmers, grooms and hunting men, all of them well used to combing this region of moorland and steep-sided valleys on horseback.

London is renowned for its open spaces, the extensive parks and sprawling commons which have been described as the lungs of the capital. During the war these areas posed a real threat to national security, as they would have been ideal spots for enemy parachutists to land in the heart of the metropolis. From May 1940, when this photograph was taken, keepers at London County Council parks and commons were trained as Local Defence Volunteers. Most of them were ex-Forces men, ideal for service in what soon became the Home Guard. Here, a sergeant from the Regular Army is instructing park-keeper LDVs in loading rifles, during a training session on a south London common.

The Port of London Authority formed its own Home Guard unit to protect the system of then thriving docks strung out along the River Thames eastwards from Southwark. Some of the men from one of these dockland detachments are seen here drawn up in a quayside parade, 30 July 1940.

This photograph, presenting an unusual – if not unique – sight on the world-famous 'floor' of the Stock Exchange in the City of London, was taken on 1 August 1940. Both the Stock Exchange Cadets and the Stock Exchange Volunteers undertook Home Guard duties designed to protect this venerable institution in the event of an enemy attack. The tension is almost palpable, as Lt Col. T.W. Towers-Clark of the Coldstream Guards casts a discerning eye over the Cadets on parade.

This is truly a case of 'babes with arms', as the Eton College section of Berkshire's Local Defence Volunteers is inspected outside the college gates, 21 June 1940. Youth and inexperience characterise this slightly ramshackle gathering, so it is daunting to think that these schoolboys were in possession of rifles and live ammunition, and at liberty to use them in deadly combination. If there were any truth in the assertion that the Home Guard was sometimes a danger both to itself and to the general public, then photographs of this kind would do little to counter that argument.

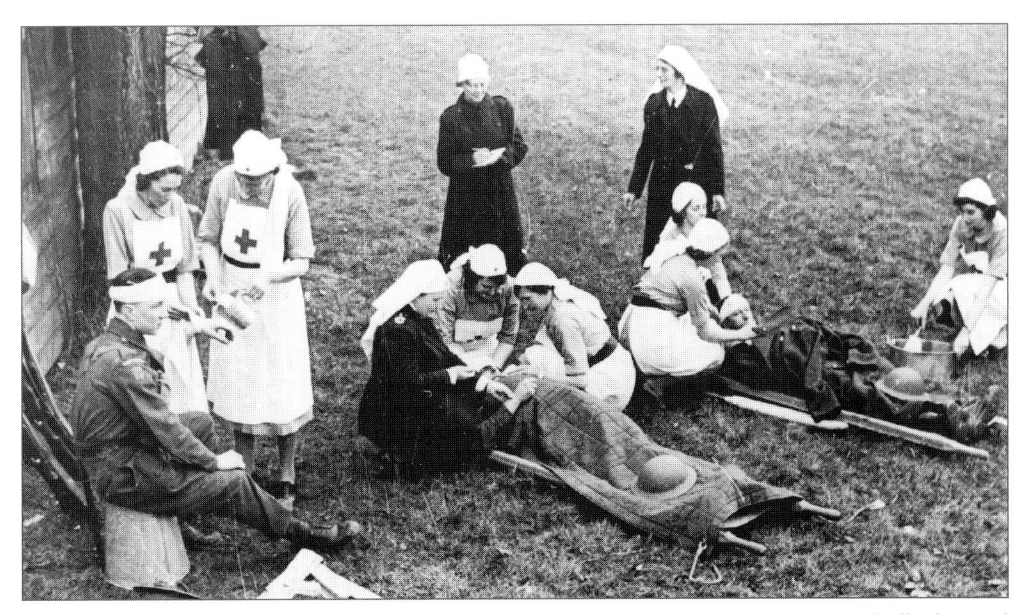

The Home Guard at Worthing in Sussex formed the first nursing unit in the country specifically designed to serve in the front line in the event of an enemy invasion. The nurses were given 'Under Fire' training alongside the men. In this photograph, dating from August 1942, a group of nurses taking part in an exercise have set up a Field Dressing Station and are tending the injured 'behind the lines'.

Pigeons were used by some units of the Home Guard to carry messages, as this photograph taken in Gloucestershire on 7 April 1942 confirms. It may seem a rather unreliable alternative to the more conventional means of transmitting information (particularly in wartime when national security was of paramount importance), but there was a case to be argued in the birds' favour. During an invasion, for example, a winged messenger might well have been more successful than a motorcycle dispatch rider in reaching its intended destination without hindrance. Messages were written on extra thin paper that was rolled into a tube and clipped to the pigeon's leg.

Dogs were also employed by the Home Guard in some areas and trained to accompany men on patrol. The most popular breeds for this type of work were alsations and mastiffs. Nell, one of the alsations selected for Home Guard duties, is seen here taking her proficiency test somewhere in north-west England, 25 July 1940. Nell, who was trained to disarm a man and retrieve his gun, is pictured bringing the weapon back to her Home Guard master. In addition to LDV armbands (by then a few days out of date), these men are clothed in the hastily distributed – and often ill-fitting – denims which preceded the issue of standard Army battledress.

The hands on knees suggest that this unusual quartet could easily be lining up to demonstrate the 1920s' dance the Charleston, whereas they are in fact part of a Home Guard roller-skating platoon undergoing speed trials in a deserted London street, 1 August 1940. The men were being trained as 'dispatch racers' by Britain's roller-skating champion Harry Lee. Apparently, they could travel at speeds of up to 40 mph on the city streets. In the event of an invasion these skaters would have had an advantage over motorcycle dispatch riders when encountering such obstacles as blocked or damaged roads, but they still couldn't beat the pigeons!

The BBC Home Guard carries out a final assault through smoke bombs, during a mock battle near Broadcasting House in central London, 9 August 1941. Norman Longmate recounts in *The Real Dad's Army* (1974) how members of the BBC Home Guard were able to get beyond the reception barriers at Broadcasting House during one exercise, with forged passes signed 'Adolf Hitler' and 'Stanley Baldwin'. Perhaps the unit had some professional actors in its midst. Whatever the case it was a formidable achievement, as anyone with business at Broadcasting House even in peacetime would confirm.

These two busmen Local Defence Volunteers, pictured here at one of London Transport's depots, are true 'comrades in arms' – and enjoying every moment of it, to judge from this photograph taken in the early summer of 1940. London Transport formed seven Home Guard battalions which, as Norman Longmate points out, 'would have fought under such stirring banners as the Camberwell Tram Depot, the Bexley Heath Trolley Bus Depot and the Dartford Country Bus Depot'. Truly, it could only have happened in the Home Guard.

Chapter Five

Parades & Inspections

The Lord Mayor of Liverpool, Alderman Sir Sydney Jones, observes members of the city's Home Guard during a training exercise, 1 August 1940. Given that this photograph was destined for public consumption in the press at the time, it is probably no coincidence that the men seen in close-up here are wielding genuine rifles. Given the national shortage of weapons among the Home Guard at this early stage, however, it is doubtful whether many of those loitering in the background would have been similarly equipped. (Clearly the first issue of Home Guard denims had yet to reach Liverpool.) Morale-boosting inspections of this kind by military, national or local dignitaries were a common occurrence throughout the war.

Col. J. Walker DSO, County Commandant of the Yorkshire Home Guard, is pictured inspecting the drawn-up ranks of the Rotherham units, 23 September 1940. (Uniforms are much in evidence by now.) Owing to the nature of local industry, this was one of those areas in the country where particularly large numbers of men were employed in reserved occupations, thereby swelling the ranks of the volunteer force. No doubt many of the Home Guards seen here worked in nearby steel mills and coal mines.

The Commanding Officer of the London District visits the Gas, Light & Coke Company at Ilford Gas Works (on the border of Essex and east London), to inspect local units of the Home Guard at work, 14 March 1944. On what appears to have been a damp and entirely cheerless day, the men are pictured here laying a minefield – demonstrating in the process that, by this relatively late stage of the war, the Home Guard had moved a long way from those early days when many of its members had paraded with broom handles.

A contingent of Home Guard motorcycle dispatch riders from Cheshire lines up on parade at Sandiway, near Northwich, with newly acquired tin hats and gas masks, July 1940. Contrary to appearances, the figure on the left is not about to conduct some kind of crowning ceremony. He is actually a police officer, giving instructions to the men on how to use their gas masks effectively.

An arms inspection of the Mobile Column, 58th East Surrey Battalion Home Guard, *c.* 1940–1, at the unit's headquarters in the grounds of Purley Cricket Club. The Mobile Column comprised mainly the youngest and most agile members of the 58th Battalion; those men, in fact, who were able to move speedily to any spot within the Battalion's defensive area, where assistance might be required to boost Company strength in the event of an enemy invasion.

Major A.R.M. Palmer (right), Commanding Officer of 'A' Company, 19th Gloucestershire Battalion Home Guard, ensures that all rifle barrels are clean and in proper working order, during a weapons inspection of the Churchdown Platoon held on Crickley Hill, near Gloucester, *c.* 1942. Given the somewhat naive, if not casual, attitude towards lethal weapons that was occasionally abroad among the Home Guard's rawest recruits, one can't help feeling that men in Major Palmer's position took something of a risk when peering so closely into the end of a rifle barrel.

Members of the Bridlington, Yorkshire (East Riding) Home Guard parading through the town in the autumn of 1944. The columns – drawn from units at Sewerby, Reighton, Speeton, Flamborough and other villages near Bridlington – are pictured here moving slowly along Kirk Gate on their return to Battalion Headquarters at the Drill Hall in Swindon Street. The men had just attended Church Parade at Bridlington's Priory Church (glimpsed in the background), and all eyes are turned left in this photograph towards the units' saluting base.

A Home Guard parade of post office employees from Brentford, Isleworth, Hounslow and Southall in Middlesex wends its way through London's Regent's Park, 1 October 1944. Here, all eyes are turned to the right as the salute is taken by Major C.J.K. Monteith. One former member of Hounslow Telephone Exchange Platoon, attached to the 21st City of London Battalion Home Guard, recalls that all the men in his unit were telephone engineers. Their job was to guard the Telephone Exchange should any German parachutists drop in unannounced. The engineers possessed not only hand grenades and rifles, but also two heavy axes with which to cut all the telephone cables before they retreated.

The Cheshunt (Hertfordshire) Platoon of the 25th Middlesex Battalion Home Guard, seen here during a Battalion parade in Town Park, Enfield, Middlesex, 1941. The left-hand file is headed by Sgt Howard, centre file by Cpl Wilson and right-hand file by Sgt Turk. The platoon's defence area was at Wormley, between the A10 and the Lea Navigation river. The defence consisted of an anti-tank ditch, and several small strongpoints made out of sandbags which platoon members filled up at nights and weekends when they were not training. According to one former member of this platoon, 'if Jerry had landed they would have taken us out before breakfast, but I like to think we would have tried our best'.

A parade of the Castleford, Yorkshire (West Riding) Home Guard, held on the town's Castlefields ground in 1941. Thomas Mangles is pictured third from the front of the right-hand file, but only two other men can be identified: Jack Clarkson and Ellis Powell. The Castlefields pub is glimpsed in the background, and a distant railway signal hints at the Leeds–York main line on the extreme left of the photograph.

An unusually large contingent of Home Guard members is shown here drawn up in the town centre at Doncaster, in what is now South Yorkshire, 1941. The passage of time has drawn a veil over the reason for this gathering, but the presence of a band (left) and a cleric confirms that a religious service of some kind was in progress. Perhaps it was one of the events held around the country to mark the Home Guard's first anniversary.

Members of Lochgelly Home Guard Platoon near Cowdenbeath, Fife, taking part in a parade through the streets of Lochgelly. The event was designed as a recruitment exercise to encourage local men to join the Home Guard. A significant proportion of the platoon members was employed at the now defunct Lochgelly Iron and Coal Company, and so were exempt from National Service owing to their reserved occupation in the coal industry. The star turn of this photograph, however, must surely be the magnificent horse which has the unenviable task of drawing along the heavily laden cart.

No. 21 Platoon, 'E' Company, 5th Gloucestershire Battalion Home Guard, pictured during a 'Wings for Victory' parade at Hartpury near Gloucester, 6 May 1944. The salute was taken by Battalion Commander Lt Col. Davenport (left) and the parade was led by Lt Hiam. Those identified here are Sgts Hamblin, Gough and Blake, Cpl Price, L/Cpl White and Ptes Harris, Banks, Nelmes, Hamblin, Smart and Howell. Comprising men from Hartpury, Ashleworth and Maisemore, No. 21 Platoon's main defensive tasks were the river bridge at Maisemore and the ferry crossing at Ashleworth. The Platoon Headquarters was at Hartpury's Parish Hall.

The men of 'C' Company, 66th Yorkshire Battalion (West Riding) Home Guard make their way along Greenhill Avenue in the suburbs of Sheffield, after attending Church Parade at St Chad's in the city's Abbey Lane, *c.* 1941. The column is just approaching Company Headquarters at the Sheffield Transport Sports Ground, which had been requisitioned for use by the Home Guard as it provided ample indoor and outdoor facilities for storage and training exercises.

This open-air church service, conducted from a draughty makeshift pulpit and attended by members of the 17th City of London Battalion Home Guard, was held among the ruins of bomb-stricken Moorgate on 29 September 1941. The battalion was composed of staff employed by the London and North-Eastern Railway Company. The salute was taken by Brigadier J. Whitehead, and the Lord Mayor of London also attended the occasion – although he is not visible in this throng.

Col Fitzgerald, Commanding Officer of the East Lancashire Home Guard, is seen here inspecting some of the units drawn from local collieries during a march past and review held on 3 September 1940.

During a visit to West Wickham in Kent, on 10 August 1940, King George VI (centre, background) inspected detachments of the local Home Guard as they were put through their paces. By its very nature the Home Guard could not hope to compete with the Regular Army in terms of fitness but, as this photograph shows, at least some attempt was made to keep limbs supple among the force's older members. All the men pictured here going through a sequence of physical jerks are over forty-five years of age.

The Rochdale Home Guard Band, photographed in 1943 during the town's 'Minden Day' parade (an event held to commemorate the Battle of Minden in 1759). The band proved extremely popular in the town, often appearing in parades and also playing in several local parks on Sunday afternoons. The musicians' repertoire included everything from military marches to Gilbert & Sullivan. On Christmas Day morning the Home Guard Band invariably toured Rochdale, playing carols and hymns. On one occasion members competed in the national brass band competition held at Belle-Vue, Manchester.

The band of the 38th London Battalion Home Guard playing outside Croydon Parish Church in Surrey for an Old Comrades' Parade, 7 November 1943. The conductor (extreme left) was Sgt S. Foster, who had brought the musicians together and lived in nearby Thornton Heath.

Joseph Christopher ('Kit') Hoggarth, photographed on parade with his young son David in the garden of their home at Crathorne in North Yorkshire, June 1941. At that time most little boys probably wanted to be engine drivers when they grew up, but it seems that David was planning to join the Home Guard. Fortunately, the need for his services would have disappeared long before he reached his teens. 'Kit' Hoggarth served in the Home Guard (initially as a Local Defence Volunteer) throughout the whole of its existence, as a member of No. 1 Platoon, 20th Battalion, The Green Howards Home Guard. Neighbouring villages which (together with Crathorne) came under the Battalion Headquarters at Yarm were Kirklevington, Castle Levington, Picton and Worsall.

CHAPTER SIX

WEAPONS & WEAPON TRAINING

The grenade section of Evershed & Vignoles Home Guard, Chiswick, attached to the 7th County of London Battalion, are pictured with the trailer carrying their Northover Projector and training stores. Live ammunition practice for this west London factory Home Guard unit took place initially in Richmond Park and, later, at ranges in Harrow and Chiswick. The Northover Projector (named after its designer, a Home Guard officer called Major H. Northover), was a cumbersome and erratic weapon, which consisted basically of a hollow metal tube resting on a tripod. Nevertheless, more than 8,000 Northover Projectors were in use with Home Guard units by the summer of 1941.

Thinking along the same lines as their colleagues in Chiswick, this group of Home Guards from Southwick (near Brighton) in Sussex increased their mobility with a light carrier trailer, which could be hitched to the back of a car or a bicycle, or even hauled by hand with the greatest of ease. The trailer could be loaded with a Northover Projector or a machine-gun and, given its extreme mobility, it was always ready for action in the case of an emergency.

Not to be outdone, members of the Ransome, Sims and Jefferies Home Guard at Ipswich, Suffolk, built their own trailer for a Browning .300 heavy machine-gun (for use against enemy aircraft). All the men were employees at the firm's Orwell Works in the town. Among those pictured here in 1940 are Cpl West, Paddy Longford, Ernie Pinkney and Richard Coe.

This demonstration in the art of throwing a Molotov cocktail was given to the Home Guard in Liverpool by Regular Army personnel, August 1940. Although there were a variety of similar home-made devices employed by the Home Guard (all subsequently outlawed), the standard Molotov cocktail – named after the Russian Foreign Minister of the day, Skriabin Molotov, and comprising a glass container filled with phosphorous, petroleum and rubber latex – was used widely during training exercises. Officially described as the No. 76 Self-Igniting Phosphorous Grenade, it was designed to be thrown against enemy vehicles and to explode on impact. Like much Home Guard weaponry, however, it was less than perfect.

In a new slant on the old Civil Service maxim, 'If it moves file it', perhaps this photograph could be captioned 'If it moves fire at it'! Here, a small group of civil servants from the Ministry of Supply Home Guard can be seen during firing practice with Lewis guns on the ranges at Wormwood Scrubs, west London, 18 March 1941. Most, if not all, government departments had been swift to react to War Minister Anthony Eden's plea in May 1940, by forming their own LDV and – later – Home Guard units.

More civil servants drawn from the ranks of another government ministry in London are learning how to handle their newly issued rifles under the expert guidance of a Regular Army Guardsman, 5 June 1940. Here, the group of novices is being shown the correct way to bring the rifle to the shoulder. One hopes – given the squad's manifest inexperience – that these weapons were not loaded. However, it is a stark reminder of just how imminently an invasion was feared at the time, to see men in suits bearing arms outside their office windows.

Bayonet practice at Carshalton, Surrey, 16 March 1941. In the early, largely weaponless days of the LDV, the term 'bayonet' was often applied loosely to describe what might only be in some cases a broom handle with an ordinary kitchen knife strapped to one end. A former London LDV recalls that he was once detailed to guard a busy entrance to Oxford Circus tube station in the heart of the West End, with no more than this makeshift device to protect both himself and his country from marauding invaders! Of course, the men shown in this photograph are wielding the genuine article.

A group of Local Defence Volunteers, watched by an attentive audience, practise their rifle-shooting skills close to the pit-head at Manvers Main Colliery near Wath Upon Dearne, in what is now South Yorkshire, June 1940. A former member of this group recalls that some of the men were issued with dummy wooden guns at first owing to the severe shortage of weapons throughout the country, and much use would they have been in the event of an enemy invasion. On this occasion, however, it seems that these fledgling marksmen are properly equipped for the job in hand.

Clearly fascinated by the subject, a member of the North Belfast Home Guard (in civilian dress) takes an interest that is possibly too close for his own good in the complexities of a petrol bomb, during a demonstration of the uses for this and similar types of anti-tank devices that was given to local units in the city by an officer from the Regular Army on 7 September 1940.

The machine-gun section of No. 4 Platoon, 'A' Company, 16th Sussex Battalion Home Guard, is pictured during a weekend of weapon training on the South Downs above Lewes, June 1943. The machine-gun was brought into action under the command of Sgt Alex Briggs (far left), and the only other member of the group who can be identified is L/Cpl John Payne (second right). According to a report of the weekend's proceedings in the local press, 'all those taking part exhibited a keenness which was an example to every Guardsman, and Col H.W. Styles [the Battalion's Commanding Officer] was well pleased with all that took place'.

M.C.D. Cordeaux, wearing sergeant's stripes on his Home Guard uniform here (but a Captain in the First World War), surveys the horizon with a Vickers machine-gun from his vantage point on the roof of a garden air-raid shelter at Northam, on the coast of north Devon. The two garden chairs, redolent of lazy summer afternoons, belie the serious purpose of the man sitting beside them, with his gun trained towards the Bristol Channel.

Lt Gen. Sir Roland Adams (centre), Commanding Officer of 'C' Northern Command, watches as two members of the Home Guard practise firing a Lewis gun during his tour of inspection of local Derbyshire units, 18 March 1941. Standing second on the left in the main group is Capt. Lord Remnant with, on the right, Brig. Gen. E.C. Walthall, Commandant of the Derbyshire Home Guard.

Two young girls gaze inquisitively, as well they might, at a member of the 1st East Lothian Battalion Home Guard as he operates a Northover Projector – once cruelly but accurately described as a drainpipe on legs – during exercises on the beach to the west of North Berwick's harbour. (Bass Rock can be seen in the far distance.) Lying on the Firth of Forth, to the east of Edinburgh, North Berwick and the adjacent coastline were considered highly vulnerable to a seaborne invasion.

The South Downs above Seaford, between Eastbourne and Brighton, provide walkers with wonderful views of the Seven Sisters cliffs and other scenic delights. Here, members of the machine-gun section of Seaford 'B' Company, East Sussex Home Guard are seen shattering the peace of those same downlands while undergoing weapon training with Vickers guns in September 1944.

Men of the Churchdown Platoon, 'A' Company, 19th Gloucestershire Battalion Home Guard, engaged in firing practice during platoon exercises on Crickley Hill, near Gloucester, *c.* 1942. Crickley Hill, one of Gloucestershire's most distinctive landmarks, was a favourite haunt of the troubled local poet Ivor Gurney, and the windswept heights provided an ideal location for Home Guard exercises. Now, in more peaceful times, the hill is a country park with an information centre, special interest trails and guided walks.

Armourer-Sergeant D.E. Paget of 'C' Company, 66th Yorkshire Battalion (West Riding) Home Guard, pictured during firing practice at the Sheffield Transport Sports Ground ('C' Company's Headquarters). Sgt Paget is using a P.17 .300 single-shot rifle which, by fitting a discharger cup to the end of the barrel as seen here, was easily transformed into a mortar capable of unleashing a No. 36 grenade (known to old hands as the Mills bomb). In those circumstances the weapon's firing position would not be as shown, but rather with the butt of the rifle resting on the ground and the barrel pointing skywards.

The Spigot Mortar team of the Sevenoaks, Kent, Home Guard, photographed during a demonstration on the Vine Cricket Ground, Sevenoaks, 1943/4. (One of the platoon's main duties was to guard 'Botany Bay' bridge on the Sevenoaks–Holborn railway line.) Officially known as the Blacker Bombard, and named after its inventor Lt Col. L.V.S. Blacker, the Spigot Mortar possessed a short barrel. The weapon could fire a 14 lb bomb in the region of 800 yards and a 20 lb bomb just over half that distance. It was an ungainly piece of equipment – a highly whimsical contraption, in fact, whose name and appearance suggest that it might have been more comfortably employed in the rough-and-tumble of the English Civil War rather than in Britain's mighty struggle with Hitler's Germany. With the Home Guard's trademark ability to 'make do and mend', many units devised and built their own trailers to haul the apparatus from one location to another. Although the Spigot Mortar came widely into use with Home Guard battalions throughout the country (nearly 20,000 were in service by 1943), more than one ex-member of the force has complained of its unpredictability when firing, coupled with a daunting lack of accuracy in the field.

A morale-boosting press photograph dating from September 1940, and bearing the caption 'This is the spirit which Hitler would never understand.' Wonderfully illustrating the mood of the country at that difficult time, a heavily armed Home Guard detachment undergoes bayonet drill at a municipal recreation ground on the south-east coast of England, while a group of four indomitable ladies, oblivious to the incongruous nature of the proceedings, quietly enjoy their game of croquet in the background. No doubt they had been playing together for years, and not even the threat of an enemy invasion was going to deter them.

Frank Earl, a member of the Churchdown Platoon, 'A' Company, 19th Gloucestershire Battalion Home Guard, prepares to throw a live grenade during platoon exercises on Crickley Hill, near Gloucester, *c.* 1942. Although there were no reports of any accidents on this occasion, Mr Earl was engaged in a potentially risky business, as more than one member of the Home Guard suffered serious injury or – in extreme cases – was killed when faulty grenades exploded prematurely.

Members of the Windermere waterborne section of the 9th Westmorland Battalion Home Guard (seen here on dry land for once) take a well-earned break during weapon practice at the firing range situated off the Crook road between Bowness and Kendal. Those pictured in this group are B. Tyson, B. Stoker, K. Kirkbride, A. Perry, H. Pattinson, T. Gilbey, Mr Musgrave, T. Woodward, P. Eleray, B. Tyson, F. Edmondson, R. Singleton, Mr Martindale, J. Clark, B. Brenand and J. Clark.

This table of exhibits set out on display at the Home Guard training school at Osterley Park, Middlesex, looks harmless enough, but it contains Molotov cocktails, hand grenades, gelignite and dynamite; just a few of the missiles and materials that would be employed against an invading force. Among the motley array of devices that were used in Home Guard training at various times, the 'sticky bomb' was possibly the most lethal to handle. Designed to be physically attached to a target rather than thrown, premature explosions sometimes occurred before the user had time to retreat. Several Home Guards were either injured or killed in this manner.

Chapter Seven

Training Exercises & Manoeuvres

Men of the Home Guard in North Wales were used to regular exercises in the mountains, and were subjected to some tough training among their native hills. Here, on 15 September 1942, during a climb to the summit of Tryfan among the peaks of the Glyder and Carnedd ranges in the Snowdonia National Park, a Home Guard is making his way across the notorious Devil's Kitchen with the aid of a rope suspended between the two walls of rock on either side. Below him is a drop of over 400 ft.

A pill box at Winchcombe, Gloucestershire. Pill boxes in a variety of designs can still be found dotted around the country today. They were used by the Home Guard mainly as training posts, but some were also employed occasionally as ammunition or weapon stores, and camouflaged so that would-be invaders might remain blissfully ignorant of their whereabouts. The simple intention was that, in the event of an invasion, members of the Home Guard would man their pill boxes and impede the progress of the enemy by firing from inside these makeshift strongholds.

Alex Wright of the Signals Section, 'D' Company, 53rd Essex Battalion Home Guard, is seen using a 'Chinese' telephone at St Leonard's Farm, Nazeing, during platoon exercises in 1941. The leather-cased field telephone being operated here was just one of many that were rescued from the cargo of a bombed vessel in the River Thames (the telephones were destined for Chiang Kai-Shek's army – hence their nickname). These instruments made communication considerably easier for Home Guard members when training exercises were held westwards from Nazeing Common, Essex, to the River Lea near Broxbourne, Hertfordshire, a few miles away.

From late 1940 Home Guard units throughout the country buckled down to some serious training in order to equip themselves for whatever lay ahead. In this photograph, dating from April 1942, Home Guards in Newcastle-upon-Tyne are being trained in methods of house-to-house fighting as a means of prizing out the enemy from hiding. On this occasion smoke bombs have been placed in the doorway of one of the houses to add to the effect of the exercise. (Needless damage was not caused, as the properties in question had already been scheduled for demolition.)

A Home Guard exercise in the streets of Guildford, Surrey, May 1942. Although the fear of spies, saboteurs and German parachutists lurking around every corner had receded to some extent by this time (the imminent invasion of May 1940 not having materialised), Home Guard vigilance was maintained and platoons spent a good deal of their time 'fighting' each other in mock invasion exercises, to keep themselves up to the mark in the event of the real thing. Here, two defending Home Guards have enterprisingly commandeered a press photographer's car to use it as cover during the proceedings.

A mock invasion exercise held at Tilehurst on the outskirts of Reading in Berkshire, May 1942. Members of the local Home Guard are defending property with Tommy guns during a street fighting exercise. This became a widely practised form of training within the force, as it was felt that the Home Guard would probably have most to offer in close-quarters engagement of this kind. Indeed, such was the importance placed on this technique that the War Office set up a Home Guard street fighting school in Birmingham.

This Home Guard street fighting exercise was held in Bedford, June 1942. After a successful 'attack' by local platoon members, 'prisoners' (one of them dressed up as a German officer) are being brought out of a deserted building in the town. This photograph (like many others in these pages) has all the hallmarks of a set-piece, designed for publication and intended to promote the Home Guard in a positive light.

Whatever inadequacies may have been attributed to its members over the years, the Home Guard was certainly not short on realism when it came to conducting training exercises and manoeuvres. Battalion commanders clearly paid great attention to detail on such occasions, as these photographs dating from June 1941 and taken during a realistic 'battle' in the City of London demonstrate. Home Guard members drawn from several London battalions had 'invaded' the square mile of the City, while sections of the GPO Home Guard (presumably from GPO Headquarters in nearby St Martin's-le-Grand) were given the task of defending the area. The mock battle is in full swing (above) as the dome of St Paul's Cathedral rises defiantly out of the rubble and devastation that surround it. Below, as a part of their own field training, several Red Cross nurses are attending to Home Guard 'casualties' of the battle at a temporary First Aid Post set up among the debris of bomb-damaged buildings close to the action, while a member of the local Civil Defence team looks on.

Armoured vehicle 'invaders' raise their hands in surrender and are ruled out of the action during a Home Guard exercise near Northampton, July 1941. Certain strict conventions governed these occasions (the rules were enforced by an umpire) and if you were 'killed' during battle you had to stay 'dead'. Apparently this was not always a disadvantage if your demise coincided with pub opening hours! A former Home Guard recalls that, having been 'shot' during an exercise, he was making straight for his 'local' when the platoon commander passed him. 'Are you dead, corporal?' the officer barked. 'Yes sir,' the man declared. 'I wish to hell *I* was!' came the heartfelt reply.

Affording much needed open space for training in the heart of the capital, not even London's royal parks were immune to Home Guard exercises (they were also ideal locations for anti-aircraft batteries), and it is hardly surprising that the rows of deck-chairs pictured here are devoid of occupants, as platoon members wearing foliage for camouflage and using seats and litter baskets for cover, attack the 'enemy' in Hyde Park, June 1941. Later, Hyde Park was to be London's focal point for the Home Guard stand-down, when 7,000 men attended a final parade held there in December 1944.

During a chilly training exercise on the Essex/Suffolk border, Jack Cornell of Bulmer (near Sudbury) gives a light to fellow Home Guard Tom Radley, who has obviously been trying out some skis in the East Anglian snow of February 1942. Perhaps the skis were an attempt to increase the local unit's mobility in the adverse weather conditions. The Home Guard, after all, was renowned for its pragmatic style of problem-solving, with carrier-pigeon messengers and a platoon of roller-skaters being fine examples of this original approach. Nevertheless, it was an aspect of the force which unavoidably engendered a few wry smiles among the population at large.

Members of Harry Lee's roller-skating platoon were trained to use Tommy guns while wearing their skates, as it was felt that the men's added mobility would be of great advantage in rounding up invaders. This photograph, taken in London during August 1940, shows a Home Guard 'on wheels' (left) attacking one of the 'enemy' (right), and wrenching a Tommy gun from his grasp. A part of the method of attack was for the Home Guard skater's right foot to clamp down on his opponent's ankle. Amusing though it may appear, the manoeuvre (if ever executed) would have inflicted great pain.

Motorcycle dispatch riders from Home Guard units throughout Cheshire gather at Sandiway, near Northwich, in July 1940 to undergo special training exercises on their machines while wearing gas masks. It would no doubt take some practice before these motorcyclists could travel safely at speed while wearing this unfamiliar apparatus. As the group of interested bystanders suggests, the Home Guard men presented quite an unusual spectacle on this occasion.

Men from the City of Lancaster Battalion Home Guard held this exercise in August 1941. It was designed to locate 'invaders' who had arrived clandestinely by parachute in nearby open countryside. Here, after being rounded up, a 'suspect' is led away under armed escort for interrogation. The bayonet pictured on the left was a fearsome weapon, designed for use in combat at close quarters. However, there is no sign of the much hated (and short-lived) pike: a length of metal tubing with a sword blade attached, which served as a bayonet and was issued to Home Guard units around this time.

Two members of the Hull Home Guard tackle various ways of demolishing a bridge in order to delay invaders, during an exercise held in September 1941. As vital crossing points for roads, railways and rivers, bridges would have been of considerable strategic importance to both defenders and attackers. However, destroying them might easily have caused more disruption for the native population than inconvenience for the enemy. Most Home Guard training exercises were conducted during the evenings or, depending on their scale, at weekends.

This photograph, taken on 12 July 1940 in the grounds of the Home Guard training school at Osterley Park, near Hounslow in Middlesex, illustrates the wrong way to stop the occupants of a car in order to examine the driver's identity papers. The two men seen lying on the ground have obviously approached the car without benefit of sufficient cover. As a result, they have been knocked down and are having their rifles taken from them by a passenger in the vehicle. This was an important training lesson, as most LDVs and – subsequently – Home Guards were involved at one time or another in road checks of this kind, during their relentless pursuit of spies and saboteurs. The training school was founded at the beginning of July 1940 (this photograph dates from the earliest days of its existence) on ground loaned for the purpose by Lord Jersey. The intensive two-day courses in guerrilla tactics and fieldcraft that were held there, usually over a weekend, became an immediate success with members of the force, who were put through their paces under the experienced eye of people like Tom Wintringham, one of the school's founders and a veteran of the Spanish Civil War. Within just a few months of its opening, several thousand men had benefited from training at Osterley Park. Later, after the school had been taken over by the War Office, Home Guard courses at Osterley Park were brought to an end. Instead, a number of smaller establishments were opened around the country, designed to provide training along similar lines for members of the Home Guard, including one at Denbies on the edge of Dorking in Surrey, and others at Amberley and Burwash in Sussex.

A contingent of the 11th Cornwall (Newquay) Battalion Home Guard seen during training on the opening day of the assault course at East Wheal Rose, St Newlyn East, near Newquay, 3 January 1943. Those taking part comprised officers and NCOs who had already received some training at nearby Trerice. This assault course and the training centre at Trerice were each the first of their kind to be set up in Cornwall by any Home Guard battalion.

A platoon from the 1st East Lothian Battalion Home Guard pictured during training on the seafront to the west of North Berwick's harbour, close to the town's golf course. It was hot work for a fine day, and the men's activities attracted much attention from visitors and townspeople gathered in the background. It is easy to forget that most Home Guards also had full-time jobs, and would squeeze in their Home Guard duties and training at nights and weekends, leaving them little free time to spend with their families at home.

Food was an essential part of Home Guard weekend training exercises, as in this case when members of the 1st Gloucestershire Battalion gathered at Seven Springs near Cheltenham, 1944. Left to right: Pioneer Colour Sgt T.D. Burford, Pte R. Whiting, Cook/Sgt A.W. Frowen, Capt. L.G. Holloway, Lt C.G. Pearce, RQMS J.C. Loud, Pte G.H. Chappel. Preparing meals on a large scale in the open air, with only the most primitive means for cooking at your disposal, requires a particular kind of skill, and it was said that Cook/Sgt Frowen was able to conjure up excellent fare in even the most adverse weather conditions.

A contingent of the Port of London Authority Home Guard holds a training exercise from a barge in the West India Docks, October 1941. Until some years after the Second World War, when the bulk of trading activity moved further downstream to Tilbury, the series of docks stretching along the Thames from Southwark to Woolwich teemed with in- and out-going vessels. The Home Guard unit formed by Port of London Authority employees, and comprising men who were intimately acquainted with this stretch of the river, kept vigil around the clock in a bid to protect the highly vulnerable docks from enemy action.

Local Home Guard members acting as German parachutists have 'landed' on the roof of the town's railway station during an exercise at Leigh-on-Sea, Essex, July 1941. Meanwhile, employing surprise tactics, an armed sergeant from another nearby platoon has daringly scaled the wall of the building and forced the 'enemy' to surrender. The plan worked well in theory here, but what would have been the result had the invaders been genuine? Opinions differ, of course, but it is difficult to believe that in general the Home Guard would have caused anything more than considerable irritation to the enemy had German forces arrived in earnest.

Taken at Woolwich in south-east London during September 1943, this photograph shows the lighter side of Home Guard training. The 4th London Battalion Home Guard organised a sports meeting in which all events were also open to members of the Regular Forces and Civil Defence personnel. Here, a group is going through its paces on a makeshift assault course, watched by a large crowd enjoying the late summer sunshine.

Training on a modest scale with members of the Aslackby platoon, 'D' Company, 4th Kesteven Battalion Home Guard near Sleaford, Lincolnshire. The group is being put through its paces in the playground of the village school. Although the photograph is undated it was probably taken in 1940, as several of the men are still not in uniform while others have apparently not been issued with rifles. This is a reminder of those early days when some Home Guard members attended parades or exercises bearing broom handles, pitchforks and wooden guns.

Members of Lochgelly Home Guard near Cowdenbeath, Fife, pictured during one of their weekly training nights in the playground of Lochgelly East School, where the platoon carried out its marching and rifle drill. The group has congregated on the lorry that was one of the platoon's main forms of transport. It belonged to Sergeant-Major McCulloch, who had a garage in Lochgelly at that time. Richard Smith, who provided this photograph, is sitting at the front (second left) holding a Sten gun. The Lochgelly Home Guard was attached to the Black Watch Battalion, and members wore that regiment's badge in their caps.

Cpl Ted Turville of the Signals Section, Churchdown Platoon, 'A' Company, 19th Gloucestershire Battalion Home Guard, keeps in touch with platoon members by battery-operated radio during a training exercise on Crickley Hill, near Gloucester, *c.* 1942. The radio seen here was known simply as a No. 38, and was usually employed over short distances. The platoon also possessed a larger radio set – a No. 19 – which was carried on the back. It had a much longer range and would have been ideal for use during full-scale manoeuvres.

Left to right: Home Guards James Brown, James ('Nobby') Clark and Robert Kelly of Dagenham, Essex, are practising their aiming technique before setting off on a training exercise at nearby Heathway station, late 1940. The station was to be attacked by a group of German parachutists (ably impersonated by a company of Irish Guards), with the local Home Guard defending the area. James Brown (who supplied this photograph, which was taken at the rear of Standfield Gardens, Dagenham, on the morning after an air raid) recalls that the Home Guard was 'wiped out' during the exercise in question.

Members of the War Office Home Guard 'attack' the Admiralty building during an evening invasion exercise held between the two government departments in London, 31 July 1941. However, the men seen here are not entirely convincing in their military role. Three members of this uninspiring quintet seem to understand what is required of them but, of the pair without rifles, one appears to be leaning unconcernedly against the fence while the other (third left) is vaguely crouching in an unconvincing manner (reminiscent, perhaps, of the LDV's early nickname 'Look, Duck and Vanish'!)

Local Home Guard units assemble in a farmyard at Dunton Bassett, Leicestershire, to consult Ordnance Survey maps and to receive an early morning briefing on the plan for the day ahead, before setting out on a large-scale training exercise in the surrounding countryside, 30 March 1943. On this occasion, these dispatch riders were detailed to play the invading force who had been ordered to secure bridgeheads and other strategically important points, while the 'panzer troops' seated in the lorry (and enjoying a last few moments' rest before the action) would attempt to repel them.

Members of the 19th London Battalion Home Guard in north-west London search a 'German' parachutist after capture, during an exercise held on 5 April 1943. Much emphasis was given at home to the fact that the enemy might arrive in disguise; parachutists decked out as clergymen, nuns, children's nannies and the like were to be fully expected. Yet, despite the Home Guard's otherwise impressive degree of realism during training, this possibility seems to be rarely reflected in scenes like that pictured above (and designed for public consumption) where, as usual, the 'prisoner' is clad in an easily recognisable uniform.

Home Guard members 'bomb' (or comb) moorland near Hartlepool, to root out 'enemy' parachutists who are believed to be hiding in the area under cover, during a training exercise held on 1 September 1941. Rural and urban environments would each have presented their own special challenges to the Home Guard in the event of an invasion. Whereas street fighting and house-to-house combat might well have been the order of the day for Home Guard units in towns and cities, open country of this nature would have demanded a vastly different approach.

An evening exercise on Windermere in the Lake District, with members of the waterborne unit of the 9th Westmorland Battalion Home Guard, *c.* 1941. The heavily armed men are seen leaving two of the unit's vessels, *Merlin* and *Josaphine*, and going ashore at Rawlinson Nab by Low Cunsey on the western side of the lake, where the wooded slopes of the Furness Fells to the south of Esthwaite Water would have provided ample cover for enemy parachutists landing in the area.

A group of Home Guards, attending a weekend camp 'somewhere in England', keep at a safe distance after exploding a land mine used to destroy a tank that was attacking a pill box, during a training exercise held in September 1941. This was another press agency photograph destined for newspaper publication at the time (hence the geographical anonymity), and doubtless designed to bolster public confidence in the Home Guard's capabilities.

We are all too familiar with unwelcome pitch invasions disrupting sporting events these days, but this affair was staged by the Swanley and Orpington Home Guard in Kent during an exercise held on 7 September 1941. Taken unawares, spectators attending a village cricket match near Orpington were thunderstruck when 'German' parachutists swarmed over the pitch while the game (being played in aid of the Cray Valley Hospital) was still in progress. 'Ground troops' with imitation tanks and anti-tank weapons added to the general confusion.

Sometimes it must have seemed like all work and no play to the men of the Home Guard. This group was undergoing training on New Year's Eve 1941 at the Burwash Fieldcraft School in Sussex, one of the War Office's successors to Osterley Park in Middlesex. The course embraced camouflage training, instruction in cooking and field sanitation, and how to make bivouacs out of ground sheets; anything, in fact, that would help to sustain the men over long periods of duty out of doors. Here, Home Guards learn how to take advantage of natural cover when stalking the enemy in open country.

A heavily posed (and not entirely convincing) encounter, in which members of an anti-tank section of the Leicestershire Home Guard capture their first home-made 'Nazi' Whippet tank during an invasion exercise held in Leicester, late 1940. It is hardly surprising that the tank's progress was arrested, as it seems incapable of much – if any – movement. Meanwhile, several of the men who have scaled the tree to propel grenades or other missiles from the protruding branches appear to be in imminent danger of falling headlong on to the shoulders of the 'ground troops'.

Another safe landing, as these hardy souls from the Beckenham Home Guard in Kent impersonate German parachutists, during a demonstration of methods for dealing with unwelcome sky invaders, 2 July 1941. The men wore all the necessary clothing and equipment for the exercise, including parachutes (seen here being inflated by a strong wind). Appearances can be deceptive, however, as there was one vital ingredient missing from the equation: the men's feet had never left the ground.

These men from the 13th Kent Battalion Home Guard are not toiling up a steep gradient in the Snowdonia range nor even one of the Lakeland fells, but they would probably have been hard-pressed to tell the difference during this mock battle exercise held in March 1944 when, as a part of the day's activities, they were required to scale a cliff face near Rochester. Using a rope to assist their climb, they expected to confront the 'enemy' (in the form of another local Home Guard platoon) once they had eventually reached the summit.

CHAPTER EIGHT

ON & OFF DUTY

"Warriors brave, go gaily forth . . . to fight!"

As the skull and crossbones etched on each of the tin helmets denotes, these four men were engaged in potentially dangerous work. The group, belonging to 'C' Company, 66th Yorkshire Battalion (West Riding) Home Guard, served as a demolition party whose job it was, at the end of each firing practice in remote areas of the Derbyshire moors, to locate, make safe and dispose of any misfired ammunition which had failed to explode. David Paget (who supplied this photograph) is on the extreme left of the group.

Filling sandbags was probably one of the most tedious jobs that a Home Guard was ever faced with (akin, perhaps, to sewing mailbags at Her Majesty's pleasure!), but it was one of those essential tasks at which everybody – well, almost everybody – took a turn. Sandbags were used widely by the Home Guard, particularly during weapon training and exercises, and also to protect points of defence. These two men, between them armed with a shovel, bags and a plentiful supply of sand, are busily filling their quota in Sussex, October 1940.

Three armed members of the Diss Home Guard in Norfolk keep watch for unwelcome intruders outside a local water tower. Left to right: Noel Madgett, Mr Voss, Albert Green. Typical of the apparently harmless but in fact highly sensitive installations that it fell to the Home Guard to protect throughout the war, water towers would have been vulnerable to attack in the event of an invasion. The pollution or long-term disruption of an area's water supply would have had serious consequences for local inhabitants. One former north London Home Guard with a sense of humour reported to me that he had guarded a water tower in Wembley for most of the war '. . . and it didn't get away once'!

Three men in search of a boat! Here is a reminder that not all Home Guard duties were confined to the relative comfort of dry land, as this trio from the Upper Thames Patrol Home Guard set out on a tour of inspection along their particular stretch of the river, 10 March 1943. This is an unfamiliar view of the UTP, whose members were more usually seen afloat rather than uncomfortably up to their knees in water.

Members of 'A' Company, 5th Glamorgan (Barry) Battalion Home Guard spend an off-duty moment together in the age-old fashion, with a pint and a cigarette. Left to right: Staff Sgt F.C. Rees, CSM R.G. Totterdell, Idris Jones, -?-, 2nd Lt E.E. Clarke, F. Jenkins, A. Bumford. 'A' Company manned an anti-aircraft gun – christened 'Oscar' by the unit – in Porthkerry Park on the outskirts of Barry. 2nd Lt Clarke's daughter recalls that it was not unusual for the men to arrive home with their caps full of mushrooms after a spell on night duty.

Brothers Cpl F.C.B. Milham and Sgt R. Milham (centre) together with other members of the Minster Platoon, Thanet Battalion, Kent Home Guard, enjoy a well-earned 'cuppa' in front of the cow shed at Ebbsfleet Farm near Ramsgate during a Sunday morning training session. The area in question is less than 30 miles from France, and was in range of the German large guns near Calais. The beaches and cliff tops were the Regular Army's domain, while the Home Guard's duties included mounting watch from Minster church tower for parachutists and downed aircrew, and guarding any crashed aircraft until they were removed.

A vaguely Churchillian figure surrenders his civilian identity papers to be checked by a vigilant senior pupil at Wellington College, 1940. Wellington College (like Eton and public schools around the country) had been swift to establish its own Home Guard platoon based on the school's Officer Training Corps (OTC). One former pupil recalls that boys of sixteen and seventeen patrolled the college grounds at night with loaded rifles.

26

G.S. Publications

338

NOT TO BE PUBLISHED

The information given in this document is not to be communicated, either directly or indirectly, to the Press or to any person not holding an official position in His Majesty's Service.

HOME GUARD

INSTRUCTION No. 15—1940

COMMON GERMAN MILITARY EXPRESSIONS

English	*German*	*Pronunciation*
Halt ! Who goes there ?	Halt ! Wer da ?	HARLT. VAIR DAR ?
Hands up !	Hände hoch !	HENDER HOCH.
Come closer !	Kommt hierher !	KOMMT HEAR-HAIR
Surrender.	Ergebt euch	AIRGAYBT OICK.
Do not shoot.	Nicht schiessen	NICKT SHEESSEN.
Throw down your arms.	Waffen hinlegen.	VAFFEN HIN-LAYGEN.
Stand still.	Stehen bleiben.	SHTAYEN BLYBEN.
Go in front of me.	Vorausgehen.	FOR-OWSE-GAYEN.
Forward !	Vorwärts !	FOR-VAIRTS.
At once !	Sofort !	SOFORT.
Double !	Marsch ! Marsch !	MARSH MARSH.
Faster !	Schneller !	SHNELLAIR.
Slower !	Langsam !	LUNGSUM.
Left !	Links !	LINKS.
Right !	Rechts !	WRECHTS.
Stop !	Halt !	HARLT.
Come back !	Kommt zurück !	KOMMT TSOORICK.

NOTE.—The pronunciation given in Column 3 is the nearest English equivalent to the German sounds. The exact pronunciation can only be learned from a German speaker.

Prepared under the direction of
The Chief of the Imperial General Staff.

THE WAR OFFICE,
20th September, 1940.

Printed under the Authority of HIS MAJESTY'S STATIONERY OFFICE
by William Clowes & Sons, Ltd., London and Beccles.

G. 254.—2438. (9/40). 180M.

Home Guard Instruction No. 15 was issued to all units on 20 September 1940, and listed common military expressions in English and German that might prove helpful to Home Guards while on duty. A rough guide to the German pronunciation was also given. Starting with the familiar 'Halt! Who goes there?', the list runs through a gamut of victorious commands before concluding on a plaintive note, 'Stop! Come back!' The document (which must have caused some amusement in the ranks) points out that the exact pronunciation could only be learned from a German speaker. Presumably you had to capture a German soldier and ask him to teach you the expressions before being able to implement the 'Instruction'.

Members of the Home Guard were not paid for the time they devoted to the defence of their country, although eventually a subsistence allowance was implemented of 1*s* 6*d* per head for periods of continuous duty lasting more than five hours, and 3*s* for over ten hours, to compensate them for any out-of-pocket expenses. These men pictured collecting their money (and an issue of boots, apparently) were photographed in September 1940, but the location went unrecorded because of wartime security restrictions. There is scant evidence of uniforms here, and the LDV armband worn by the man in the foreground was out of date by this time.

Mr N. Simpson, a member of the mounted Home Guard unit that patrolled the North Yorkshire Moors, is pictured here on duty, 8 August 1940. Mr Simpson was a farm foreman by day and a Home Guard at night. All the members of this mounted squadron were first-class horsemen with an unrivalled knowledge of the surrounding country. The corps was raised by a former Sheriff of York, Mr Thompson, and was well supported in the local community. The extensive and solitary moors would have afforded ample cover for enemy landings by parachute, or for invaders arriving by sea along the adjacent coastline from Scarborough to Redcar.

An unpalatable photograph of a Home Guard wife trying her hand at aiming and sighting a rifle on the South Downs in Sussex, watched by off-duty members of the local platoon relaxing in the autumn sunshine, October 1940. Tales of accidents and fatalities resulting from the misuse of firearms abound in the annals of the Home Guard. It is quite possible that the rifle being wielded here was loaded, causing the photographer to flirt unnecessarily with death or severe injury. It is a foolhardy scene altogether, given that there are children in the vicinity.

"*Warriors brave, go gaily forth . . . to fight!*"

This cartoon drawn by Lt Col J.C.T. Willis appeared in an amusing little book called *Home Guard Rhymes*, written by Lt A.H. Watkins and published in 1943. The caption reads: 'To those poor Home Guard "widows"/Who sit alone at night/And wait, while we, their warriors brave/Go gaily forth to fight.' There was an impression generally shared by the more sceptical of Home Guard wives that their menfolk spent a large proportion of their time in the pub while out on nightly Home Guard business, rather than actually mounting patrols or doing guard duty. How this uncharitable notion got abroad remains a mystery.

Patrolling the wild places of Britain could be a solitary – not to say dangerous – business, and there is tension in the air as this member of the mounted Home Guard on Dartmoor keeps an armed watch for unwelcome intruders during a spell of duty on Middle Tor to the south-west of Chagford, Devon, 30 July 1940. Somewhat fancifully, perhaps, this lone horseman so obviously intent on scanning the distant horizon reminds me of 'stout Cortez' who, in a poem by John Keats, watched '. . . silent upon a peak in Darien'.

A light-hearted moment for John Patterson of the Ulster Home Guard. Mr Patterson was a member of 'B' Platoon at Buckna in County Antrim, which met for training every Thursday evening under the command of Lt Robert (Bob) Davison. The men were transported by the Regular Army to shooting ranges at Glenwherry and Slevenee for firing practice. Contrary to appearances, 'B' Platoon was not a mounted unit, nor is there any suggestion that the donkey was the platoon's only form of transport!

Home Guard dispatch rider John French photographed outside the Half Moon pub in Plumpton, East Sussex, while on duty *c.* 1940–1. Mr French was a member of the local platoon that met every week for drill and instruction in the parish hall at Plumpton Green (the railway line running between Lewes and Burgess Hill divides the two villages). His job was to take messages by motorcycle to Ditchling, the next big village only 3 or 4 miles distant to the west.

The grave of Cpl George Beveridge, a bomb instructor with the Burnley Home Guard in Lancashire. Cpl Beveridge died in October 1944 following an accident on duty, when a grenade he was handling during training exploded without warning. (His platoon colleague Sgt George Bagley was seriously injured.) Cpl Beveridge was one of 1,200 Home Guards thoughout the country who were killed by one means or another in the line of duty; a statistic which may shock many people whose only knowledge of the Home Guard has been gleaned through the long-running BBC comedy series, *Dad's Army*.

Chapter Nine

Special Occasions

King Haakon of Norway, the so-called 'people's king', visits the Bristol Aeroplane Company at Filton, *c.* 1942, attended by a Guard of Honour provided by the 13th Gloucestershire (City of Bristol) Battalion Home Guard, and watched by an enthusiastic crowd. All the men in this battalion were employed in the company's Bristol Aero Engine Department. Eventually, the 13th Gloucestershire Battalion (the largest in Bristol) was split into two, with the additional unit being known as the 18th Battalion and stationed in BAC's Aircraft Department. The British version of Concorde was assembled at Filton by the British Aircraft Corporation during the 1960s and 1970s.

Members of the Lindfield Platoon, on the outskirts of Haywards Heath in Sussex, are among the guests enjoying a celebration VE Day dinner held in honour of the Home Guard at the King Edward Hall, Lindfield, 1945. (Note the quart bottles of the local Tamplin's Brown Ale arranged along the tables, rather than the wine that would be commonplace today.) The Home Guard men had long been out of uniform by the time this photograph was taken, but most units came together again to celebrate the end of the war in Europe.

The massed ranks of the 11th Cornwall (Newquay) Battalion Home Guard march through the streets of Newquay during a Battalion parade held on 16 May 1943. Platoon parades were a common occurrence and Company parades were not unknown, but days when the whole Battalion paraded as one unit were rare indeed. 'Some difficulty was experienced in actually finding a parade ground that would safely accommodate 1,200 officers and men', the Battalion Handbook explains, 'but eventually the Gresham's School Sports Ground on Newquay's Golf Links was chosen'. The men formed into columns and set off on a 2-mile march through the town. They are seen in this photograph passing their Battalion Headquarters where the salute was taken by Mr G.H. Johnstone, the Civil Defence Controller for Cornwall. Later a religious service was held on the Golf Links, and afterwards Battalion members gave demonstrations of First Aid and gun drill. 'Hot, tired and thirsty,' the Battalion Handbook concludes, '. . . we had given Newquay something to think about. The 11th Cornwall Battalion, that had been born when the skies over Britain were so dark, had not wasted its time since those difficult days.' The Battalion was – and remains – known as 'The Choughs', named after the bird found in Cornwall reputed to be 'gentle and peace-loving but which knows how to look after itself should the need arise'. In 1943 the Battalion formed a Home Guard Association also called 'The Choughs', one of the very few such clubs still in existence today. Initially it boasted more than 1,000 members but by the mid-1980s there was less than half that number. Although the passing years have inevitably reduced membership still further, an annual dinner is held in February at a Newquay hotel.

This unusual photograph was taken through an archway at Buckingham Palace, and shows the 2nd County of London (Victoria, Chelsea, Kensington) Battalion Home Guard, during the mounting of the King's Guard on 13 May 1944. It was an auspicious occasion, held as one of the events marking the Home Guard's fourth anniversary. The men seen here were subjected to three weeks' special training at Chelsea Barracks prior to the great day, under the eagle eye of Drill Sgt J. Barker of the Coldstream Guards.

There are not many public figures in the world who could be so easily identified from a rear view alone, but the posture and tell-tale beret easily give the game away. Monty (later 1st Viscount Montgomery of Alamein) is inspecting members of the village Home Guard platoon at Longparish, near Andover, Hampshire. The men are gathered outside Upper Mill with Monty (centre) and Major General G.P. Dawnay (left). Monty held the Home Guard in great esteem, and used his influence in high places to help maximise the force's potential.

This conference marking the second anniversary of the Home Guard was held in May 1942, and was attended by some of the force's most senior figures drawn from its various Commands. Left to right facing camera: Col. G.F. Perkins, Lt Col. S.M. de Whatten, Maj. Lord Denham, Col. J. Whitehead, Col. A.J.H. Dove, Maj. Gen. Viscount Bridgeman DSO, MC, (Director-General of the Home Guard), Col. J.A. Lonemore, Mr G.F. Calton (War Office Principal), Capt. Hon. H. Douglas-Home and Maj. D.V. Smith. There was a considerable amount of highly desirable public relations and morale-boosting mileage to be gained by holding a range of events each year around the time of the Home Guard's formation. On the first anniversary, in May 1941, members from selected London units were allowed to mount guard at Buckingham Palace, a rare honour that was accorded to the Home Guard again on several later anniversaries. The following year King George VI highlighted the occasion by assuming the title of the Home Guard's Colonel-in-Chief, thereby lending further credibility to the force by his royal patronage. Successive anniversaries were marked by designated 'Home Guard Sundays', large parades in central London and throughout the country, special messages broadcast on the wireless by the King and Prime Minister, and demonstrations mounted by Home Guard units the length and breadth of the land.

King George VI inspects members of the local Home Guard at Callow Hill, Virginia Water, Surrey, during a break in field exercises held *c.* 1942–3. This would not simply have been a public relations stunt on the King's part (or what might in today's terms be dubbed a 'media opportunity'). By agreeing to be the Home Guard's Colonel-in-Chief, a title he assumed once again in the force's post-war incarnation, King George VI had clearly demonstrated his commitment to, and support for, Britain's 'civilian army'.

During a visit to West Wickham in Kent, King George VI watches detachments of the local Home Guard in their early days of training, 10 August 1940. (Note that the man seen to the left of the King is still wearing an LDV armband, and is clad in denims rather than the battledress which came later.) Here, the King sees messages being received and dispatched at a heavily camouflaged observation post. Royal visits of this kind would have considerably boosted the morale of the men concerned.

Members of a Home Guard First Aid Team in Croydon, attached to the 32nd Surrey Battalion Home Guard, are pictured here in 1944 with the winner's cup following their success in a county First Aid competition. The group includes Jim Moat, L/Cpl Fred Booker, Pte Charles Curtis and Dick Short. 'Should it ever be my misfortune . . . to be injured by enemy action or in any other way,' enthused the Battalion's Medical Officer, 'may it be my good luck to fall into their competent hands.'

The official naming ceremony for the Home Guard's own London, Midland and Scottish locomotive was performed at one of the capital's main line railway stations (probably Euston) on 30 July 1940, by Lt General Sir Henry Pownall KBE, CB, MC, Inspector-General of the Home Guard. Both the driver and fireman of the engine were members of the railway's own Home Guard section. Lord Stamp, the Chairman of LMS, is shown pointing to the nameplate following the end of the ceremony, which was held barely a week after the Local Defence Volunteers had officially changed their name to the Home Guard.

One of the events held around the country to mark the Home Guard's third anniversary in May 1943 involved members of the Ford Works Home Guard Band, which was made up entirely from men employed in the vast car factory at Dagenham, Essex. The band was selected to appear in the popular BBC wireless programme called 'Listen to the Band' (there is still a programme of that name in the BBC's radio schedules today). Here, the musicians and band committee are pictured after an anniversary Church Parade held in Dagenham following the broadcast.

The 22nd Yorkshire Battalion (West Riding) Home Guard Band from Brighouse, pictured on the steps of the War Memorial by the Alhambra Theatre, Bradford, after appearing in a charity concert on the same bill as the famous singing duo, Anne Ziegler and Webster Booth. Among those seen in the front row are Bandmaster Thomas Hunter (centre, wearing peaked cap), Kenneth Beaton, Frank Longbottom, Arthur Boothroyd and Irvine Longbottom. Fred Wright is in the centre of the group behind his big drum. The band won prizes on several occasions during the war years at the annual brass band competition held at Belle-Vue, Manchester.

Alderman E.J. Denton christens Birmingham's first Home Guard Motor Patrol boat, *The Ladywood*, 19 August 1940. The vessel was destined for service on the canal system in the Ladywood area of the city, and was manned by Home Guard members who were employed in factories nearby. Representatives of local firms stand and watch as Alderman Denton breaks a bottle of wine over the bows of the Home Guard's new 'fighting ship' during the ceremony. (It seems a terrible waste of wine in a period of wartime austerity.)

Maj. Gen. Viscount Bridgeman (fifth right) visits members of Seaford 'B' Company Sussex Home Guard in his capacity as the force's Director-General. A staunch ally of the men under his overall command, Bridgeman retained his post until shortly before the stand-down in 1944 and, in the following year, he wrote as near poetically as a military man may ever get about those who had filled the ranks of Britain's 'civilian army'. 'We see on the chessboard of war', he declared, 'the Home Guard as the Castle guarding the King, while the Knights of the Regular Army went overseas in search of the King's enemies.'

The unmistakable figure of General Charles de Gaulle, accompanied by Lt Col Ernest Bowater MSM, Commander of the 32nd Warwickshire (Birmingham) Battalion of Birmingham City Transport Home Guard, inspecting a Guard of Honour in the city on 7 February 1942. Both the 31st and 32nd Battalions were usually called upon to perform Guard of Honour duties for the City of Birmingham, and they were kept busy with a succession of illustrious visitors: King Haakon of Norway in April 1942 (only two months after de Gaulle's visit); the Duke and Duchess of Gloucester in January 1943; the South African statesman Smuts and British military supremo Montgomery in 1944. When the Director-General of the Home Guard visited the Birmingham area on a tour of inspection in June 1941, after reviewing a Guard of Honour he examined various squads who put on training displays for his benefit at the Recreation Ground adjoining the city's Perry Barr Garage. According to a note in the Birmingham City Transport Home Guard Battalions' Record Book, Viscount Bridgeman declared himself 'very satisfied with what he had seen', and commented on the high standard of efficiency attained.

CHAPTER TEN

THE STAND-DOWN & BEYOND

Barely a week before the main crop of stand-down events were staged around the country to mark the official end of the Home Guard's contribution to the Second World War, members of the 5th Gloucestershire Battalion Home Guard attended a Thanksgiving parade held on 26 November 1944, at which the salute was taken by Queen Mary. The men are pictured here after the church service, drawn up in College Green beneath the walls of Gloucester Cathedral.

The 'bare ruin'd choirs' of leafless trees that form the backdrop to this photograph add a sombre note to an already poignant occasion, as members of the 5th Gloucestershire Battalion Home Guard gather in Gloucester Park for their stand-down parade on Sunday 3 December 1944. Although the Home Guard was stood down before the war was over, most of its members were probably grateful to have more free time once again to spend with their families, but there were others who felt that Britain's 'civilian army' had been dispensed with prematurely. Scenes like this were being enacted simultaneously throughout the land. In London 7,000 Home Guards marched through the West End to a final parade in Hyde Park.

Seaford 'B' Company Home Guard join together with other local units at their stand-down parade in Lewes, East Sussex, Sunday 3 December 1944, watched by a thin crowd who gathered despite the miserable weather. Meanwhile, elsewhere in the county one commanding officer was telling members of the 26th Sussex Battalion at Crawley that the stand-down did not necessarily spell the end for the Home Guard. As it turned out his comments proved hopelessly optimistic, despite the fact that the force was not officially disbanded until the end of the following year.

In the years when our Country
was in mortal danger

DAVID McCORMICK.

who served 26.6.40 to 31.12.44

gave generously of his time and
powers to make himself ready
for her defence by force of arms
and with his life if need be.

George R.I.

THE HOME GUARD

A message from the King was issued to every member of the Home Guard at the end of his term of service. As this certificate shows, David McCormick – who served with No. 1 Platoon, 'D' Company, 90th West Lancashire Home Guard in Liverpool – was a member of the force from the beginning to the end of its wartime existence.

These ladies are pictured after attending their own stand-down ceremony in King's Lynn, Norfolk, at the end of 1944. Women were not allowed to enrol as Local Defence Volunteers or Home Guards, partly because the War Office had felt that existing bodies like the Women's Voluntary Service might be adversely affected by such a move. However, in 1943 they were rather grudgingly admitted as Home Guard Auxiliaries. In the event, fewer women than had been expected took advantage of the opportunity, although the government's figures would not have included the countless numbers who were already serving unofficially as volunteers with Home Guard units up and down the land.

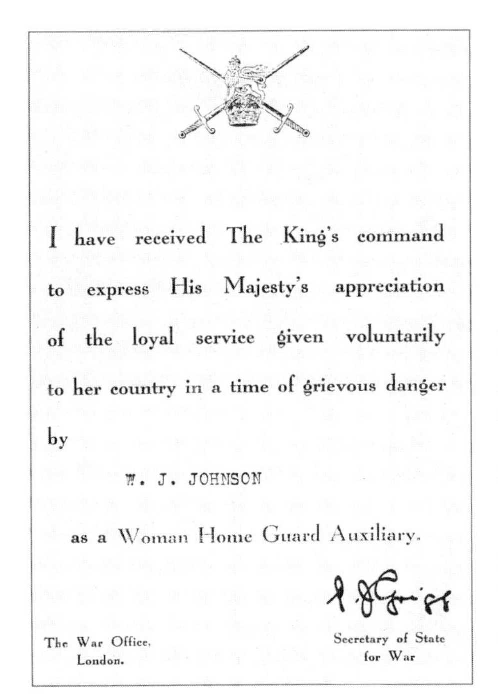

I have received The King's command to express His Majesty's appreciation of the loyal service given voluntarily to her country in a time of grievous danger by

W. J. JOHNSON

as a Woman Home Guard Auxiliary.

The War Office, London.

Secretary of State for War

A 'personal' message of thanks issued by the War Office was received by every Woman Home Guard Auxiliary at the end of her period of service. This citation was given to Miss W.J. Johnson (later Mrs Lowe) who appears in the group pictured above. One former Auxiliary in Kent, echoing a familiar tale of expectations not being realised, recalls that she was asked to take part in her platoon's mock battle one night. Quite excited by the prospect she duly presented herself on the evening concerned, was issued with a password and then cruelly disillusioned to be told that her part in the exercise was to shell the peas for the officers' meal!

Members of the Inveraray Home Guard, Argyll, gather for their final parade at stand-down, 1944. Left to right: Capt. J. Campbell-Blair, J. Rodgerson, D. MacDonald, C. MacLaren, T. Faulds, A. MacKechnie, J. MacBeath, D. MacDougall, C.A. MacArthur, T. MacPherson, R. Buntain, A. Mackenzie, A. MacIntyre, Sgt D. MacKechnie, J. Rose, D. MacLeod, J. Cook, J. Mailer, Capt. A.J. MacPherson, Sgt Welsh. During the Second World War Inveraray, on the shores of Loch Fyne, was home to a huge Combined Operations Training Centre and, as one local resident put it, 'the place was alive with troops. What these highly trained soldiers must have made of the local Home Guard is open to question, but at least they were "doing their bit".'

Officers from 'B' Company, 3rd Renfrewshire Battalion Home Guard relaxing – and no doubt pausing for reflection – outside the Territorial Army Drill Hall in Paisley Road, Barrhead, after completing their stand-down parade through the town, 31 December 1944. Those pictured here are J. Clark, J. Watson, J. Forsyth (second right), J. Small (fourth right), T. Galbraith, J. Connell (fifth left), R. Thomson (second left), D. Sorley, T. Ferguson (third right), P. Wright (first right).

When 7,000 Home Guards drawn from units throughout the United Kingdom gathered in central London for the national stand-down parade on Sunday 3 December 1944, few – if any – of them had travelled further for the occasion than the four men standing in the back row of this photograph, who were all from Shetland: Lt R.G. Anderson of Whiteness; Cpl Andrew J. Johnson of Sound; L/Cpls J.R. Mundie and James Young, both of Lerwick. Two of the men – Lt Anderson and L/Cpl Mundie – had dined as guests of the Lord Mayor of London at a banquet given in the Mansion House on the previous evening.

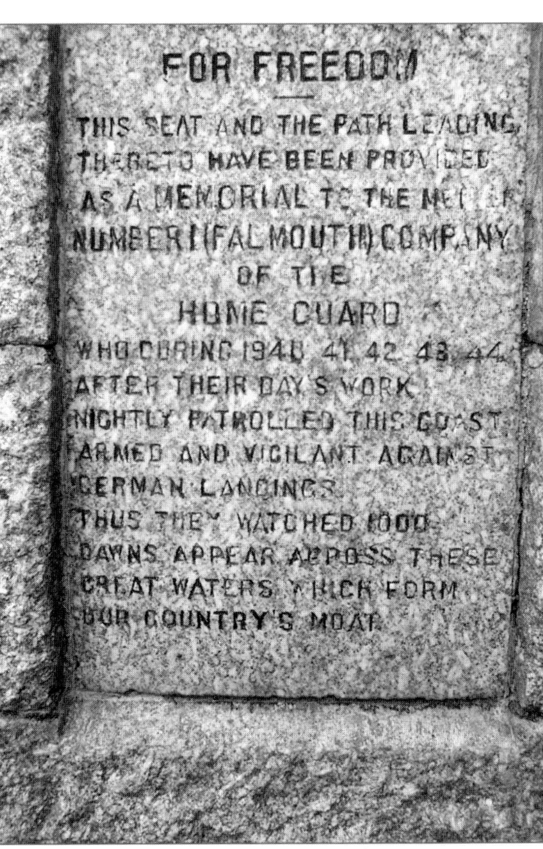

This Home Guard memorial can be found on a coastal path at Stack Point near Falmouth in Cornwall. It reads: 'For Freedom . . . This seat and the path leading thereto have been provided as a memorial to the men of No. 1 (Falmouth) Company of the Home Guard who, during the period of 1940, 41, 42, 43, 44, after their day's work, nightly patrolled this coast armed and vigilant against German landings. Thus they watched 1,000 dawns appear across these great waters which form our country's moat.'

The Home Guard was resurrected to some extent during the 1950s, largely in response to the so-called 'Red Scare' from behind the Iron Curtain. It was structured differently from its wartime predecessor and did not attract as much support. Here is the 12th/13th Somerset Home Guard Cadre Battalion pictured at Locking Road School in Weston-super-Mare. Some of the members have been identified. Back row: Sgt S. Middle, Sgt E. Mayne, Sgt R. Merrick, Sgt Shaw. Middle row: Lt W. Amesbury, Sgt Gamblin, Lt Thompson, Sgt Greedy. Front row: Capt. H. Heyburne, Major Reynolds, Col Lanyon, Capt. Evans, Lt K. Langworthy, Lt Wride, Lt Holmes.

Members of the 12th/13th Somerset Home Guard Cadre Battalion pictured at the Yoxter rifle range near Priddy (between Cheddar and Wells) in the Mendip Hills, 1952–6. Left to right: Lt K. Langworthy, -?-, Lt W. Amesbury, Capt. H. Heyburne. To keep the battalion conversant with new training methods during this 1950s revival of the Home Guard, courses were held at the Somerset Light Infantry's Taunton barracks, while field exercises were conducted around Imber on Salisbury Plain.

Schoolmasters Roger Ray (left) and Lewis Creed (right) are seen here 'defending' Warninglid Ridge in Sussex during field exercises. The men belonged to the ten-strong Handcross Home Guard based at Ashfold House, a boys' preparatory school lying between Horsham and Haywards Heath. The unit was formed in 1952 and disbanded four years later. Had the platoon ever been called into action (which it was not), then support would have been forthcoming from other Home Guard units based at Crawley and various nearby towns. 'This was no ordinary Home Guard,' wrote Roger Ray. 'With training over for the night, the men would repair to the masters' club where a pint of ale and a three-course meal were waiting.' Although Britain has been involved – to a greater or lesser degree – in a number of international conflicts over the years since 1956, the need to create another 'civilian army' at home has never arisen. However, there was a brief moment during the spring of 1982 when the Home Guard might just conceivably have seen the light of day once more. The denizens of my local pub at Nazeing in Essex decided to form their own Home Guard platoon following Argentina's invasion of the Falkland Islands. However, as most people in the village agreed, the 'volunteers' had probably been looking through the bottom of too many empty glasses at the time, or watching a surfeit of *Dad's Army* on television. Needless to say, the platoon evaporated even before its first parade had been called.

It's time to pause for a sandwich and some liquid refreshment, as Sgt Maj. Batho relaxes with members of the 32nd Essex Battalion Home Guard during training on the firing ranges at Rainham Marshes, *c.* 1953–4. Enrolment figures for this post-war incarnation of the Home Guard – a force which had been essentially a wartime phenomenon, raised when an invasion of Britain seemed imminent – never really achieved their hoped-for potential in the rather different climate of the 1950s.

With the war long over and their duty done, almost the entire Signals and Intelligence Section of the Churchdown Home Guard Platoon in Gloucestershire gathers for a peacetime reunion in 1952. The men had been based at a farm in Parton Lane, Churchdown, with the church tower on nearby Chosen Hill serving as a look-out post. Formed by Sgt Hartland and including J. Franklin, R.C. Jones, J.C.M. Baker, E.R. (Ted) Turville, W.N. Perry, R. Blair, E. Cole, C.T. Cole, H. Western, J.J. Hitch and D. Davies, the unit was known officially as No. 4 Section, No. 15 Platoon, 'B' Company, 5th (later 19th) Gloucestershire Battalion Home Guard.

ACKNOWLEDGEMENTS

I am grateful to the following people who provided me with photographs and, in many cases, shared their memories of the Home Guard:

W.J. Amesbury, Mrs Jo Anscombe, H.W. Batho, Denis Bedford, R.W. Bennet, Mrs Jennifer Bentley, Richard P.J. Blake, Mrs Betty Blanchfield, Mrs P.G. Booker, Colin L. Bowater, Mrs Margaret Bromwich, James Brown, Frank Bryant, Ron Butterworth, Richard Coe, Lewis Creed, J.A. Cutland, Mrs Joan Daniells, Mrs E.Y. Davies, G.E. Emery, T.J.T. Ferguson, L.D. Foreman, Mrs Dorothy French, Miss J. Green, Dennis Grew, W. Griffin, Mrs Maureen Griffiths, Dr K.E. Hinrichsen, Adrian Hoare, Bob Hoggarth, T.C. Hudson, Mrs H.S. Hunter, H. Hurrell, Stella J. Jarvis, George Kent, G.J. Lamplough, Mrs V. Lancaster, R. Langford, Mrs S.M. Lovell, J. Lowe, David McCormick, Mrs Rae MacGregor, Capt. M.F. Milham, G. Munn, Mrs Vera Nicholls, Derek Norris, D.E. Paget, Fred C. Patrick, John Patterson, John Payne, Alan G. Pickering, Mrs N. Price, Ethna Rafferty, Gordon Reynolds, J.N. Rodd, A. Shanks, J.A. Simmons, H.G. Smith, Mrs Mary Smith, Pat Smith, Richard Smith, J. Stovold, Mrs Muriel Sudbury, Mrs Grace Symons, Tony and Shirley Trinder, Rodney Tulloch, E.R. Turville, Ron Underwood, Maj. P.J.R. Waller, David W. Ward, Mrs S.E. Warren, C.D. Waters, G. Weatherstone, W.A. Webber, Peter White, Mrs D.M. Woodward, Alex G. Wright, David C. Younger. Photographs on the following pages appear with permission of the Trustees of the Imperial War Museum, London: pp. 1, 7, 9 (bottom), 10, 12 (top), 14, 30, 31, 32 (top), 34, 35 (bottom), 36, 37, 38, 39, 41, 43, 44, 45, 46, 47, 48, 49, 50, 52, 53, 59 (bottom), 60, 64 (bottom), 65 (bottom), 66, 67 (top), 68 (top), 69 (bottom), 73 (top), 74 (bottom), 76 (top), 78, 79, 80, 81, 82, 83, 84, 85, 87 (bottom), 88, 91, 92, 93 (bottom), 94, 95, 96, 98 (bottom), 100 (top), 103, 104 (top), 105 (top), 111, 112 (bottom), 113 (bottom), 114 (top), 115 (top).

Every effort has been made to trace the copyright holders of photographs used in this volume. Any omissions are unintentional, and I would be pleased to include further acknowledgements (upon notification) in any future edition of this work. I should like to acknowledge the financial assistance of the Authors' Foundation in awarding me a grant during the preparation of this book. I am also grateful to Rose Carroll and Bernadette Walsh for their support and encouragement throughout the entire project.

BRITAIN IN OLD PHOTOGRAPHS

Aberdeen
Acton
Amersham
Annandale

Around Bakewell
Balham & Tooting
Barnes, Mortlake & Sheen
Barnet & the Hadleys
Barnet Past & Present
Bath
Beaconsfield
Bedfordshire at War
Bedworth
Belfast
Beverley
Bexley
Bideford
Bilston
Bishop's Stortford & Sawbridgeworth
Bishopstone & Seaford II
Blackburn
Bletchley
Bloxwich
Braintree & Bocking at Work
Brentwood
Bridgwater & the River Parrett
Bridlington
Bristol
Brixton & Norwood
Buckingham & District
Bury
Bushbury

Camberwell, Peckham & Dulwich
Cambridge
Cannock Yesterday & Today
Canterbury Cathedral
Canterbury Revisited
Cardigan & the Lower Teifi Valley
Around Carlisle
Castle Combe to Malmesbury
Chadwell Heath
Cheadle
Chelmsford
Cheltenham in the 1950s
Cheltenham Races
Chesham Yesterday & Today
Around Chichester
Chiswick & Brentford
Chorley & District
Around Cirencester
Clacton-on-Sea
Around Clitheroe
Colchester 1940–70
Coventry at War
Cowes & East Cowes
Around Crawley
Cromer
Croydon
Crystal Palace, Penge & Anerley

Darlington at Work & Play
Darlington II
Dawlish & Teignmouth
Around Devizes
East Devon at War
Dorchester
Dorking Revisited
Dumfries
Dundee at Work
Durham: Cathedral City
Durham People
Durham at Work

Ealing, Hanwell, Perivale & Greenford
Ealing & Northfields
The Changing East End
Around East Grinstead
East Ham
Around Eastbourne
Elgin
Eltham
Ely
Enfield
Esher
Exmouth & Budleigh Salterton
Farnborough II
Fleetwood
Folkestone II
Folkestone III
The Forest of Dean Revisited
Frome
Fulham

Galashiels
Around Gillingham
Gloucestershire at Work
North Gloucestershire at War
South Gloucestershire at War
Goudhurst to Tenterden
Grantham
Great Yarmouth II
Greenwich
Greenwich & Woolwich

Hackney II
Hackney, Homerton & Dalston
From Haldon to Mid-Dartmoor
Hammersmith & Shepherd's Bush
Hampstead to Primrose Hill
Around Harrogate
Harrow & Pinner
Hastings & St Leonards
Hayes & West Drayton
Around Haywards Heath
Around Helston
Around Henley-on-Thames
Herefordshire
Around Highworth
Hitchin
Holderness
Hong Kong
Huddersfield II
Huddersfield III

Ilford to Hainault
Ilfracombe
Ipswich Revisited
Islington
Jersey III

Kendal Revisited
Kensington & Chelsea
East Kent at War
Keswick & the Central Lakes
Kingston
Kirkby & District
Kirkby & District II
Kirkby Lonsdale
Knowle & Dorridge

The Lake Counties at Work
Lambeth, Kennington & Clapham
Lancashire
The Lancashire Coast
Lancashire Railways
East Lancashire at War
Lancing & Sompting
Leeds in the News
Around Leek
East of Leicester
Leicester at Work
Leicestershire People
Letchworth
Lewisham & Deptford III
Lincoln
Lincoln Cathedral
The Lincolnshire Coast
The Lincolnshire Wolds
Liverpool
Llandudno
Around Lochaber
Theatrical London
Loughborough
Lowestoft
Luton
Lye & Wollescote
Lympne Airfield
Lytham St Annes

Around Maidenhead
Manchester
Manchester Road & Rail
Mansfield

Margate II
Marlborough II
Marylebone & Paddington
The Melton Mowbray Album
The History of the Melton Mowbray Pork Pie
Merton, Morden & Mitcham
Middlesbrough
Around Mildenhall
Milton Keynes
Minehead

The Nadder Valley
Newark
The Norfolk Broads
Norfolk at Work
North Walsham & District
Northallerton
Around Norwich
Nottingham Yesterday & Today

Oldham
Ormskirk & District
Otley & District
Oxford Yesterday & Today
Oxfordshire at Play
Oxfordshire at School
Oxfordshire Yesterday & Today

Penwith
Penzance & Newlyn
Around Pershore
Peterborough
Around Plymouth
Poole
Portslade
Prestwich
Putney & Roehampton

Redditch & the Needle District
Richmond
Rickmansworth
The River Soar
Around Rotherham
Royal Norfolk Regiment
Rugby & District II
Ruislip
Around Rutland
Around Ryde

Saffron Walden
St Albans
St Andrews
Salford
Salisbury II
Sandhurst & Crowthorne
Sandown & Shanklin
Around Seaton & Sidmouth
Sedgley & District
Sedgley & District II
Sheffield
Sherwood Forest
Shoreham-by-Sea
Lost Shrewsbury
Southampton
Southend-on-Sea
Southwark, Bermondsey & Rotherhithe
Southwark, Bermondsey & Rotherhithe II
Southwell
Stafford
Around Staveley
Stepney, Bethnal Green & Poplar
The History of Stilton Cheese
Stockport
Stoke Newington, Stamford Hill & Upper Clapton
Stourbridge, Wollaston & Amblecote
Stowmarket
Stratford, West Ham & the Royal Docks
Streatham II
Stretford
Stroud & the Five Valleys
Stroud & the Five Valleys II
Suffolk
Suffolk at Work II
Sunderland
Sutton
A Swindon Album
Swindon III

Around Tamworth
Along the Thames
Around Thirsk
Tipton
Tipton II
Around Tonbridge
Torquay
Around Truro
Twickenham, Hampton & Teddington

Uley, Dursley & Cam
Upminster & Hornchurch
The Upper Fal
Uxbridge 1950–1970

Ventnor

Wallingford
Walsall Revisited
Waltham Abbey
Walton-on-Thames & Weybridge
Wandsworth at War
Around Warwick
Weardale
Weardale II
Wednesbury
Wembley & Kingsbury
West Wight
Weymouth & Portland
Around Wheatley
Around Whetstone, Totteridge & Finchley
Whitchurch to Market Drayton
Wigton & the Solway Plain
Willesden
Wimbledon
Around Windsor
Wisbech
Witham & District
The Witney District
Wokingham
The Women's Land Army
Woolwich
Worcestershire at Work
Wordsworth's Lakeland
Wotton-under-Edge to Chipping Sodbury

SUTTON'S PHOTOGRAPHIC HISTORY OF TRANSPORT

Jaguar
Jensen & Jensen-Healey
Lotus
Morgan
Rolls-Royce
TVR
Vauxhall
Suffolk Transport
Manchester Road & Rail
Manchester Ship Canal
Black Country Railways
Cheshire Railways
Derbyshire Railways
Devon Railways
Lancashire Railways
Shropshire Railways
Warwickshire Railways
Worcestershire Railways
Steam around Reading
Steam around Salisbury

To order any of these titles please telephone our distributor, Littlehampton Book Services on 01903 828800
For a catalogue of these and our other titles please ring Emma Leitch on 01453 731114